T0032315

# HOW TO GRIEVE

# ANCIENT WISDOM FOR MODERN READERS

■ ■ ■ ■ ■

For a full list of titles in the series, go to https://press.princeton
.edu/series/ancient-wisdom-for-modern-readers.

# HOW TO GRIEVE

■ ■ ■ ■ ■ ■

An Ancient Guide to
the Lost Art of Consolation

Inspired by Marcus Tullius Cicero

*Translated and introduced
by Michael Fontaine*

PRINCETON UNIVERSITY PRESS

PRINCETON AND OXFORD

Published by Princeton University Press
41 William Street, Princeton, New Jersey 08540
99 Banbury Road, Oxford OX2 6JX

press.princeton.edu

Library of Congress Cataloging-in-Publication Data

Names: Cicero, Marcus Tullius. | Fontaine, Michael, translator.
Title: How to grieve : an ancient guide to the lost art of consolation /
inspired by Marcus Tullius Cicero, translated and introduced by
Michael Fontaine.
Description: Princeton : Princeton University Press, 2022. | Series: Ancient
wisdom for modern readers | Includes bibliographical references.
Identifiers: LCCN 2021059581 (print) | LCCN 2021059582 (ebook) |
ISBN 9780691220321 (acid-free paper) | ISBN 9780691220338 (ebook)
Subjects: LCSH: Consolation. | Grief. | Bereavement. | Tullia, active 1st
century B.C. | Cicero, Marcus Tullius.
Classification: LCC BF637.C54 C6613 2022 (print) | LCC BF637.C54
(ebook) | DDC 152.4—dc23/eng/20220225
LC record available at https://lccn.loc.gov/2021059581
LC ebook record available at https://lccn.loc.gov/2021059582

British Library Cataloging-in-Publication Data is available

Editorial: Rob Tempio and Chloe Coy
Production Editorial: Sara Lerner
Text Design: Pamela L. Schnitter
Jacket: Heather Hansen
Production: Erin Suydam
Publicity: Maria Whelan and Carmen Jimenez
Copyeditor: Karen Verde

Jacket Credit: Courtesy of Shhewitt / Wikimedia Commons

This book has been composed in Stempel Garamond

Printed on acid-free paper. ∞

Printed in the United States of America

1 3 5 7 9 10 8 6 4 2

For Ava and Jacob

*quos summe diligo summeque diligendos merito suo censeo*

A lush once spied an amphora emptied out
on the ground, still gasping breaths of its aroma,
the dregs remembering the noble wine.
She snorted the fragrance up her nose and sighed:
"O lovely ghost! What goodness surely once
you had within, if *this* is what's left over!"

—Phaedrus, *Fable* 3.1

■ ■ ■

*Vellem igitur Ciceronem paulisper ab inferis
surgere.*
I wish, therefore, Cicero would for a short time
rise from the dead.

—Lactantius, *Divine Institutes* 3.13

■ ■ ■

*Quas natura negat, praebuit arte vias.*
And for what nature denies, art has discovered
a way.

—Claudian, Preface to *Proserpina*

# CONTENTS

# ACKNOWLEDGMENTS

Times change, and not always because we want them to. When things fall apart, the Stoics, the original grief counselors, counseled fortitude.

In exploring their ideas, I would like to thank George Thomas, who writes under the name Quintus Curtius, for insight, encouragement, and advice. I also thank Tad Brennan and Charles Brittain for sharing their expertise on Plato with me, Rob Tempio for taking this project on, and my mother, Maryanne, who was a valuable sounding board from the beginning.

My greatest debt is to Alyssa. As Job said (17:12),

*Et rursum post tenebras spero lucem.*

And again after darkness I hope for the day.

ITHACA, NEW YORK

# INTRODUCTION

## The Lost Art of Consolation

After a stratospheric year as Consul, Marcus Tullius Cicero was on top of the Roman world. Five years later, that world had turned on him. He was ostracized, pressured into exile, his property confiscated or destroyed. He spent a year and a half wandering, aimless and adrift. A decade later, his wife left him. He immediately married again, but badly, and only for the money.[1]

Rock bottom, though, had yet to come. In 45 BCE, his beloved daughter Tullia died from complications of childbirth. She was only 32.

Familiar questions began to haunt him. *Is there life after death? Are our loved ones in heaven? How could things go so wrong?* And, perhaps most pressing of all, *Is there any way to recover from something as earth-shattering as the death of a child?*

The problem, as every ancient thinker emphasizes, is Fortune: luck, chance, randomness, circumstances beyond our control. Looking back three

and a half centuries later, the Christian convert Lactantius was impressed by how courageously Cicero had fought back all his life—right up to the moment he couldn't any longer:

> In his *Consolation*, Marcus Tullius says he always fought Fortune and won, in thwarting his enemies' attacks. She didn't break him even when he'd been chased from home and homeland. Then, though, when he lost his dearest daughter, he shamefully admits that Fortune has defeated him: "I give up," he says. "It's over."[2]

The death of a child can do that. It can make a person fall to pieces. As Cicero put it elsewhere (*Tusculan Disputations* 3.61),

> People whose grief is so great that they're falling to pieces and can't hold together should be supported by all kinds of assistance. That's why the Stoics think grief is called *lupe*, since it's a "dissol*u*tion" of the whole person.

In the text to which Lactantius refers, the *Consolation*, Cicero did something he later boasted no one had ever done before. "I hacked Nature," he declares, "and talked *myself* out of depression."[3]

The idea of a *self*-consolation is familiar from many later writers, from Marcus Aurelius to Augustine to Boethius. At the time, however, it was something new in world literature, equal parts philosophy and motivational speech. It seems history's greatest speaker put all his powers of persuasion to convince an audience of one—himself—to get past his grief and move on.

And, says Cicero, it worked.

■ ■ ■

*Effigiem oris, sermonis, animi mei*
She's exactly like me—face, speech, heart and
  soul.
                    —Cicero, *Letter to Quintus*, 1.3/3.3

Who was Tullia Ciceronis? As far as we can tell, she was an extraordinary woman who was born into extraordinary circumstances. Yet her life was not the fairytale it should have been.

Born in 78 BCE, Cicero's only daughter found herself widowed at age 20. She remarried at 22, then divorced and remarried again at 27, to a bad husband. That third marriage produced one stillbirth, little love, and a second divorce a few years later— while Tullia was pregnant. In January 45, at the age of 32, she gave birth to a boy, but the baby did not

live. The next month, Tullia herself died of complications at her father's country villa.

Throughout this life of disappointments, Tullia radiated strength and resilience. Cicero repeatedly praised her fortitude, and even chose a strange word to describe it: *virtus*, greatness or manfulness—a word which, thanks to its root in the word for a man or hero (*vir*), had never been applied to a woman before. Cicero saw his daughter as a hero, a saint. When she died, therefore, he was sure she was in heaven—was *up* there, looking down, happy, safe, and waiting for him. That she, and eventually he, would live forever.

All this sounds very Christian, and it is, in no small part because the Christian notion of heaven is indebted, like Cicero, more to Platonic philosophy than to the Judaism from which it sprang. Regardless of our religion, though, these thoughts will be familiar to all of us who have lost a loved one. It has always been so. In the face of unremitting misery, as the Enlightenment thinker Voltaire asked in his *Homily on Atheism*,

> what position does there remain for us to take? Is it not the one taken by all the scholars of antiquity in India, Chaldea, Greece, Rome, that of believing that God will cause us to pass from this

unhappy life to a better one, which will be the development of our nature?[4]

Moreover, like so many bereft parents, Cicero resolved to build a shrine to his beloved daughter. Unlike most, however, he wanted the "shrine" to be an *actual* shrine—a church, we would call it today— with Tullia herself literally worshipped as a god. He began making plans to make it happen.

But it never came to pass. Perhaps such plans were just a part of his grieving process.

■ ■ ■

*Fortīs Fortuna adiuvat.*
Fortune favors fortitude.

—Roman proverb
(Terence, *Phormio* 203, cited by Cicero)

"Stoicism," says Peter Breggin, "is a philosophy for someone going down in an airplane." When Cicero needed help, he was going down in an airplane. He turned to the wisdom of ancient Greece for answers.

In the weeks following Tullia's death, Cicero read and reread classic philosophical treatises on coping with grief. By his time, "consolatory literature" was an established genre. The finest examples to reach us are three letters by Seneca, a Stoic, and

two by Plutarch, a Platonist, but those all lay generations in the future. In Cicero's time, the greatest guide to bereavement—cited several times in the text translated here—was a treatise by Crantor of Soli (d. 276 BCE). That treatise is lost today, but traces of it appear in later consolatory literature by Plutarch and Cicero himself, especially his *Tusculan Disputations*, which he wrote very soon after the *Consolation*.[5] And we know enough about Crantor's treatise to realize its coping strategies and grief therapies are nothing like practices commonly recommended today.

Grieving today is collective and often analyzed as a series of stages. For Crantor, as for the Stoics who refined his ideas, it is a matter of individuals finding the inner strength to accept reality—or comforting illusions—and moving on. Cold logic will convince us that death is part of life, indeed better than life, and that we're nothing special: tragedy and loss are inherent in the human condition. Others have survived it before us, which means we can, too. Resilience, endurance, and individual effort, therefore, are the way forward.

These ideas may sound harsh and alienating. For Cicero, they were his path out of despair. After studying these models, he sat down and wrote his *Consolation* in just a matter of weeks. He had a first

draft by March 11, 45 BCE, and a final draft just a week or two later. His essay would go on to become one of the great masterpieces of the ancient world, a new standard and source of solace and relief for centuries.

...

> The reputation of your works is immense; your name is on everyone's lips; but your serious students are few, whether because the times are unpropitious or because men's wits are dull and sluggish, or, as I think more likely, because greed diverts our minds to other ends. Thus some of your books have perished, I suspect, within the time of men now living; and I do not know if they will ever be recovered. This is a great grief to me. . . . Here are the names of your lost books: the *Republic*, *On Familiar Matters*, *On the Military Art*, *In Praise of Philosophy*, *On Consolation*, *On Glory*. . . .
>
> —Petrarch, *Letter to Cicero*, 24.4 (December 1345), trans. Morris Bishop

Cicero's *Consolation* was lost in antiquity. At some point during or after the fourth century, it disappeared, leaving us no more than a dozen quotations by other authors.

In 1583, however, as the Renaissance was coming to an end in Italy, a new book quietly appeared in shops in Venice. It contained the text translated in this volume, and its title page carried a sensational announcement:

> The *Consolation* of Marcus Tullius Cicero, the book whereby he consoled himself on the death of his daughter, newly rediscovered and published.

Was it real? A forgery? A prank? Nobody knew, and nobody would say. The book contained no introduction and offered no explanation of where this treasure came from.

And its contents were astonishing. The text contained all the known fragments of Cicero's lost *Consolation* and innumerable points of contact with other relevant texts in the same consolatory tradition. It included many examples of famous Romans who endured grief, examples that Cicero had made inquiries about in contemporary letters to his friends. Much of the content matches what we find in the *Tusculan Disputations*, a text Cicero began writing very soon after. And the style itself is highly Ciceronian.

Skeptics emerged immediately, but to all appearances the text was real. For centuries it was

included among Cicero's collected works, albeit with a note indicating that many believed it was a forgery. Most scholars have come to agree with this, but defenses appeared sporadically. In 1999, a computer program was finally devised to assess stylometrics—that is, the relative frequency across a range of texts of "function" words, like *et* (and) or *in* (in) or *est* (is), to determine authenticity.[6] The computer crunched the numbers and determined that the text was probably not authentic.

It is not authentic. Despite all that effort, amazingly, in four and a half centuries no one ever bothered to fact-check a block quote attributed to Plato in section 57. Anyone who had would have learned, as did I, that it comes not from Plato but from Marsilio Ficino's popular *Life of Plato*, first published in Italy in 1477 and frequently reprinted during the Renaissance.[7] It is not clear whether that false quotation was a blunder, or (as I think) a deliberate trap, akin to the "trap streets" that cartographers include on maps to protect their intellectual property. Either way, the case is closed.

Who *did* write our treatise, then? Suspicion has traditionally devolved on the Modenese historian Charles Sigonius (Carlo Sigonio, 1524–1584). After reviewing all the evidence, I'm not so sure, though it does seem likely he knew who did—and refused to say.[8]

INTRODUCTION

It doesn't matter, though, because not all fakes are fake in the same way. *This* fake is not a fabrication, but a *recreation*. It is Cicero refined and distilled and concentrated. Some parts are taken almost verbatim from Cicero's other works, and his spirit and thought infuse the entire text. Not a word is inconsistent with his philosophy.

Furthermore, it's clear that the forger combed every single one of Cicero's philosophical essays, as well as the entire consolatory tradition, in assembling this essay. One can imagine the forger copying relevant passages onto notecards, spreading them out on a table, and then carefully assembling them into a coherent whole. The result is akin to the best historical fiction of Robert Harris.

Scholars today estimate the original *Consolation* was only around 20–40 pages long, which is to say, no more than a third to half the length of our fake one. Yet the themes it covered were identical: the therapeutic value of philosophy, the value of role models, competing views of the human condition, and belief in the immortality of the soul—especially Tullia's soul.[9] In that regard, our *Consolation* offers us a more accurate view of what Cicero probably wrote than any academic article on the topic ever could.

The resulting text is nothing short of a masterpiece of recreation and imitation. It seems to

experiment with a stream-of-consciousness style that reflects Cicero's wavering mindset. It also offers one of the most forthright reflections on the plight and hardships of women to be found anywhere before the nineteenth century.

It is no wonder, then, that despite its origins, many have found this text a source of enormous relief, and, as Cicero intended, consolation.

## A Note on the Text and Translation

The Latin text is based on Klotz 1876, though I've repunctuated it as I did in *How to Tell a Joke*. I have also suggested a few emendations (in sections 86, 122, 125, 139, 144, 189, 208, 214, and the deletion in 99). In 89, 90, and 99, I adopt emendations suggested by other scholars that are not reported by Klotz. The genuine fragments of Cicero's *Consolation* are printed in **bold** and numbered according to Vitelli's edition of 1979.

The only prior English translation is that of Blacklock 1767. Among the five French translations I discovered, I am indebted to that of Mangeart 1840 for several insightful interpretations and turns of phrase.

The subheadings in the translation are my own addition. Otherwise, notes in this edition are kept

to a minimum; readers will find a "secret decoder ring" of all the source quotations I could find — many of them handled with incredible virtuosity — and other lagniappe at http://classicsprof.com/ciceros -consolatio/

# HOW TO GRIEVE

# CONSOLATIO

## *vel* De Luctu Minuendo

[1] Quamquam recentibus morbis medicinam adhibere vetant sapientes, nihilque adversi hominibus accidere solet in vitā quod aut improvisum aut inexspectatum videatur, conemur tamen, si quā ratione possumus, mederi nobismet ipsis et domesticae subvenire calamitati.

Si enim, quotiens usu venit, consuluimus ceteris, ¿cur non aliquando nobis ipsis? et, si mala quae nec vitari nec averti humanis viribus possunt, pertulimus toleranter, ¿cur non ea, si possumus, ratione leviora faciamus? praesertim quum ad aegritudines et molestias depellendas eo acrius incumbere homines debeant quo melius est sine curā vivere quàm curis et angoribus oppressum ac circumventum, humanam condicionem—satis per se miseram—aliis etiam incommodis efficere miseriorem. [2] ¿Quid porro praestantius, ¿quid utilius est quàm quum corpore valeas, curare ut etiam animo valere possis? si quidem corpus animi gubernaculo, animus autem ministerio corporis indiget. At neque animus aeger

# WORDS OF HEALING

## On Coping with Grief

### Preamble

CONSOLATION — *SELF*-CONSOLATION — IS MY
ONLY HOPE

[1] I know the experts say not to treat *recent* traumas, and that in human life, no tragedy should
strike us as surprising or unexpected. Still, though,
I have to try—if there's any possible way—to *fix*
myself, and stop my world from caving in.

I mean, if I always counseled others when it hit,
then why *not* myself? And if I've absorbed horrors
that human strength was powerless to avoid or
avert, then why not—if I possibly can—use *reason*
to relieve them? People *should* block out heartache
and grief, block them just as fiercely as a life without worries is preferable to a prison of stress and
anxiety, or to making the human condition—hard
enough as it is—even harder with *new* problems.
[2] Besides, when you have physical health, what's
more crucial or beneficial than looking after your
mental health? The body needs the heart's gover-
nance, and the heart, the body's labor. But an aching

bene gubernabit nec adfectum corpus animi recte pare-
bit imperio.

[3] Quamobrem, prudenter a doctis et sapientibus viris
et cogitatum et factum est, qui de luctu minuendo ante
nos scripserunt; quorum exstant satis multa—sane sapienter litteris mandata—inprimisque a Theophrasto, Xenocrate et Crantore; quorum libros quúm saepe animi
causā sumpserimus in manūs, admirati eorum saluberri-
mis praeceptis refertam et condītam eloquentiam, túm
proxime lēgimus necessariò. [4] Casus enim ereptae nobis
filiae, quam in oculis ferebamus, eximiis et virtutis et prudentiae laudibus praestantem, ita nos vel perculit vel ad-
flixit ut ab iis opem ad leniendum et mitigandum dolorem
petere coacti simus, quorum maxime doctrinā atque auctoritate antea movebamur.

Itaque, multa quae ab illis vel acute cogitata vel ele-
ganter enuntiata sunt ad dolorem nostrum abstergen-
dum colligemus ut, si minus ceteros in tanto maerore de-
lectare poterimus, quod aliàs et dicendo et scribendo
efficere conati sumus et fortasse interdum praestitimus,
saltem nobis ipsis medeamur. [5] Sed nos etiam in hoc
fortiores erimus quàm ceteri, quibus difficile non fuit—
quum doloris expertes ipsi essent—alios consolari et a
maerore abducere; nos autem, dolore adflicti, consolationem a nobis petentes nosmet ipsos in dolore vincemus

heart is a poor governor, and a disabled body cannot obey the heart's directives properly.

[3] That reality demonstrates the insightfulness of those enlightened thinkers, my predecessors, who wrote about coping with grief. A number of their efforts, which they were wise enough to write down, are extant. The main ones are those of Theophrastus, Xenocrates, and Crantor, and I'd often picked their books up for fun; I admired their engaging style, witty and packed with helpful mantras.[10] Now, though, I'm reading them of necessity, [4] because the shock of seeing my daughter torn from me—my beautiful darling, a paragon of heroism and wisdom—has crushed me, devastated me. I need *help* to blunt or mask the pain, and I find myself forced to seek it from those authorities whose expertise always so impressed me in the past.

To wipe away the pain, therefore, I will collect many of their insights and quotable sayings. That way, even if I fail to please others in my grief— which on other occasions my speeches and writings have tried, and sometimes perhaps even managed to do—then at least I'll fix myself. [5] And in so doing, I'll be even *stronger* than my predecessors. They weren't grieving themselves, so it wasn't hard for them to console other people and spirit them out of mourning. *I*, however, will find consolation within *myself*: though stricken with grief,

ac naturae quandam quasi vim adferemus.

Quae ¡utinam tanti sit ut ceteros quoque in pari fortunā doceat adversos casūs patienter ferre! Qui, quo saepius contingunt, eo propiores hominibus putandi sunt, quasique in ipsā humanā naturā innati atque insiti, ideoque levius ferendi. Qui enim hominem se esse agnoscit hominisque nomen sibi vindicat, ¿cur ea quae hominis maxime propria sunt, recusare ac reiicere audeat?

Quod simul ut fecisset, et imprudens et iniustus meritò haberetur. [6] Atque hic locus a Theophrasto egregie tractatus et perpolitus est, itemque a Xenocrate, quorum uterque eos qui communes casūs recusant, imprudentiae atque iniustitiae condemnat; alter etiam dis ipsis adversos non dubitat appellare. Quod etiam gravius crimen est ac vix in homine tolerabile: qui, quum omnia dis immortalibus accepta referre debeat, quorum ope vivit, intellegit, agit, si eorum voluntati repugnet, cum dis Gigantum more bellare videbitur.

[7] Haec autem perite (ut dixi) a multis tractata sunt, sed ego **Crantorem sequor** [*V4*], cuius lēgi—brevem illum quidem, sed vere aureum et (ut Panaetio placuit) ad verbum ediscendum—"De Luctu" librum, quo acute

I will "hack" Nature and conquer *myself* amidst my grieving.

I hope this effort can show others in my situation how to endure sudden losses with forbearing, since the more often tragedy strikes, the more intimately *human* we must think tragedies are. We must think of them as virtually congenital, bound up with human nature, and hence, for that reason, easier to endure. I mean, if you accept and pride yourself on being human, then how could you possibly reject and refuse a chief condition of being human?

The moment you do *that*, moreover, you'd rightly be seen as shortsighted and acting in bad faith. [6] Theophrastus is subtle and superb on this issue, as is Xenocrates; both expose the shortsightedness and bad faith of those who bridle at life's inevitabilities. One of them even declares such people "anti-God," since theirs constitutes a heinous and wildly inappropriate stance for a human being: namely, that if instead of *thanking* for all your blessings those immortal gods who gave you life, intelligence, and action, you *fight* their decisions. It suggests that, like the Giants, you're going to war against the gods.

[7] Well, a lot of people have written about these matters carefully, as I said, but **I like Crantor**. I read his book *Grief*, and though it's short, it's solid gold. Panaetius was right: every word is worth

universam doloris medicinam complexus est—sed humanae naturae incommoda ita diligenter et accurate expressit ut quasi **luendorum scelerum causā nasci homines** [*V1*] et in hanc lucem ingredi possis agnoscere.

[8] Fac enim nasci hominem et in lucem edi: continuò
senties, non rerum humanarum dominum et guberna-
torem exortum, sed verius miseriarum servum atque incommodorum. Nam infantiam et pueritiam vagitus, lacri-
mae, imbecillitas, nullus nec rationis nec corporis usus,
dolores molestiaeque quàm plurimae amplectuntur.

Adolescentiam ardor quidam excipit aetatis—nec prudentiae nec iudicii compos—, rerum utilium ac laudabi-
lium contemptio, voluptatis et saepe turpitudinis appeti-
tio, veri boni ignoratio, in pares ferocia, in superiores
superbia, in infimos adrogantia. [9] Ex his, contentiones,
rixae, contumeliae, adsiduus denique molestiarum con-
cursus exsistit; ex rebus honestis contemptis, infelicitas et
infamia; ex turpibus curiose adreptis et conquisitis, luctus, morbi, perpetuum denique sui ipsius odium, ex
cognitā rerum turpium mercede conflatum. [10] Adde

memorizing. In it, he analyzes every treatment for grief brilliantly. Yet he also lays out the miseries of human nature so precisely and exactly that you can tell **human beings were** pretty much **born** and put into this world **to atone for sins**.

## The Miseries of Man

### THE STAGES OF LIFE

[8] I mean, picture man born and put into the world. Instantly you'll see he arrives, not the master and monarch of human affairs, but the slave of misfortune and misery. Infancy and childhood are spent in crying, tears, weakness, cognitive and physical helplessness, and infinite pain and problems.

Adolescence gets overtaken by a characteristic flush—shortsighted, headstrong—and a disdain for practicality and honor, by an eagerness for pleasure (often *shameful* pleasure), and a blind eye to what's right. It's cruel to peers, arrogant toward authority, and obnoxious to those below. [9] That attitude leads to arguing, fistfights, and verbal abuse—essentially, one headache after another. Disdain for honor begets failures and embarrassment; the freewheeling hunt for sensuality leads to grief, traumas, and endless self-loathing, all of it caused by recognizing the wages of your sins. [10] Add in the

insanas pecuniarum largitiones, nullam futuri temporis curam, non inopiae, non liberorum, non uxoris, non
posterorum, non familiae. Quae, siquis "aetatis" potius
"vitia" quàm "naturae miserias" velit appellare, quamquam
nominis quaestionem inducat, non tamen ipsas ab homine miserias atque incommoda removebit. [11] Nec
verò audiendus erit qui haec ab humanae naturae miseriis separanda putet, quòd "non in natura insita sint, sed
unius vel aliquorum hominum errores videantur;" totius
autem naturae illa esse adfirmet quae a nullo prorsus homine seiungi possunt. ¡Quasi verò humanum non sit
irasci, quòd "multi non irascantur," aut non humanum
loqui et societatem coire, quòd "multi reperiantur qui
nihil difficilius faciant quàm cum hominibus congredi
aut sermonem cum aliquo conferre"! [12] Vere autem
humanae miseriae sunt, quòd, etsi non omnes in uno,
certe omnes in omnibus et aliqua in multis et multae
saepe in uno agnoscuntur.

Iam constantis aetatis quot quantaeque miseriae sint,
non difficile est intellegere, at difficillimum enumerare.
Haec enim ex omnibus hominis aetatibus in perturbationes animi, in pericula capitis, famae, fortunarum una

lunatic blowing through money, the heedlessness of the future, of poverty, of children, a wife, posterity, your world. If you want to say those problems all stem from "your stage of life" instead of "nature," then you'll be quibbling over nomenclature, sure, but you won't do a thing to excise the miseries and problems from the man. [11] Ignore, too, anyone who thinks they must be separated from the miseries of human nature, because "they aren't congenital, no, they're failings of the *individual*, or of just some people," while claiming problems intrinsic to *Nature* are those that are absolutely inseparable from *any* man. Pfft! As if it were *not* human to lose your temper simply because *many* people don't lose their temper, or *not* human to talk and participate in society simply because you can find many people who think the hardest thing in life is getting together or having a conversation with someone. [12] They really *are* human miseries, though, since even if not all of them are attested in *one* person, they're certainly all attested in all people, and some are in many and many are often attested in one person.

When you're established in life, it isn't hard to understand the *number* or *intensity* of the miseries. It's almost impossible to list them all, though, since this stage more than any other meets with heartaches and hazards to your life, reputation, and

maxime incurrit. [13] Sicut enim ceterarum omnium aetatum ad res negotiaque quúm privata túm publica peragenda, aptissima est maximeque idonea, ita etiam una—prae ceteris omnibus—difficultatum miseriarum-que omnium quae ex publicā privatāque administratione oriuntur, particeps et socia est. Haec privata amicorum negotia procurat, haec publica sustinet munera, haec gloriam et commodum ex rebus feliciter evenientibus, haec aerumnas et molestias ex adversis experitur. Huic bonorum civium propugnatio, huic malorum accusatio proposita est, huic invidia et aemulatio a bonis imminent, a malis pericula et insidiae intenduntur: aetas numquam sibi ipsi non infesta, numquam pacata, semper laboriosa, semper anxia et sollicita. Quae si non aliquos interdum vel utilitatis vel voluptatis fructūs ex adsiduo labore perci-peret, se ipsam profectò regere ac tueri non posset. [14] Sed miseriarum numerus multo maior est; magnitudo, autem, tanta ut neminem a publicis procurationibus non avertere ac deterrere possit.

Illustre praebuit exemplum universae civitati ca-lamitas nostra, quam ex partā civium salute, ex de-fensis aris ac focis, ex proditoribus a rei publicae ac populi Romani cervicibus depulsis contraximus. Sed nostra fuerit aerumna, civibus contigerit salus

livelihood. [13] You see, of all the stages it's the one best suited for managing your wealth and private and public business, and it alone shares the headaches and problems that public and private administration give rise to. This is the stage that looks after friends' private affairs, that undertakes public service, that experiences the glory and fruits of success, and that experiences the hardships and frustrations of failure. This is the time for championing the good and prosecuting the wicked. It's targeted for jealousy and competition from the good, and for sabotage from the wicked. It's a period forever fighting itself, forever restive, always preoccupied, always anxious and obsessing. If it didn't occasionally enjoy some advantage or upside from the constant struggles, it would simply break down. [14] The downsides, however, are many more, and they're *so* miserable that they can dissuade and turn anyone off from public life.

My own fate gave the whole country a good example of that. The thanks I got for rescuing my fellow citizens, for defending their homes, and for thwarting the traitors who held a knife to the throat of the people and republic of Rome, was being hit with disaster.—I can handle the hardship, though, if it brought

et quies; quam etiam vitā ipsā profundendā, si opus fuisset, libentissime redemissemus. [15] Nihil necesse est mihi de me ipso praedicare; sed, tamen, verissime adfirmare possum eos demum annos me vere vixisse quos in praeclaro aliquo patriae vel commodo vel ornamento consumpsi, ac—si longius mihi vitam producere liceret—non me alia causa ad diutius vivendum quàm publicae utilitatis studium curaque adduceret; quae una cogitatio in homine gloriosa et laudabilis est maxime.

[16] Nunc, quae extrema de aetatibus superest, ¿quid ego de senectutis incommodis ac miseriis loquar? quas plurimas esse et gravissimas, et nomen ipsum—languoris calamitatisque plenissimum—indicat et aspectus ipse senum hominum patefacit. ¿Quid est enim aliud senem videre trementem, incurvum, canum, imbecillum, infirmum, quàm cernere morientem vivum aut viventem mortuum?

Ac si nonnullis visum est magnam esse senilis aetatis consolationem, prudentiam usu rerum quaesitam—quae illius aetatis propria est—eosdem illos fateri oportet, ex eo ipso fonte manare etiam ad senes non minimum doloris atque molestiae. [17] Qui enim se prudentem rerumque agendarum peritum agnoscit, ¿cur non doleat,

my fellow citizens security and stability; in fact I'd gladly have paid my life for them, if such had been the price! [15] There's no need for me to speak about myself, but in my heart of hearts I *can* affirm that in the years I dedicated to improving or enhancing my country, I did truly live. And, if I had the power to extend my life, *nothing* could persuade me to live longer than the pursuit and cultivation of the common good, since *that* is the single most glorious and praiseworthy project for a human being.

[16] Now as to the final stage of life, what should I say about the horrors of old age? The very name evokes languor and falling. It hints that emergencies are frequent and serious, and the very sight of old people proves it. To see an old person — trembling, stooped, timeworn, weak, frail — is that anything less than seeing a live man dying or a dead man living?

It's true that wisdom acquired from long experience is a privilege of that stage of life. If some see it as a great consolation of old age, though, they should admit that it's also a major source of heartache and pain. [17] I mean, if you *know* you're a wise and experienced leader and you see a best course of action, then how could it not upset you to see age *itself*

quae optime intellegit, prae aetatis vitio, optime etiam perficere non posse? et si patriam diligit, ¿cur non angatur, quod quam consilio iuvat, operā etiam iuvare non possit? eoque maior prudentium dolor est, quòd optimorum consiliorum fructum nullā aliā ratione percipi posse quàm si optime ad exitum perducantur intellegunt, quòd nisi vir optimus patriaeque amantissimus ad agendum accedat, prorsus inania sint futura.

[18] De aetatibus satis mihi videor dixisse. ¿Quid iam de generibus hominum loquar? ¿Aut numquid principes viros et medios et infimos aeque miseros esse negare possum?

Reges ipsi quàm miseri sint—quantoque opere sollicitudini, timori, atque insidiis propositi—satis ostendit Dionysius, quum, imminente capiti gladio Damoclem fortunae suae felicitatem voluit experiri—nec mirum, quum iis bellorum calamitates, agrorum vastationes, populorum caedes, urbium exitia immineant. [19] Quae quum eveniunt, qui victoriā potitur aliquid et ad gloriam et ad imperium semper acquirit, sed tanta praeterea rerum amissio tantusque sumptus consequitur ut magni constet victoria, ac plerùmque praestiterit numquam arma sumpsisse. Sin profligatio exercitūs aut clades aliqua contingit, nihil eo statu miserius ne cogitari quidem potest, siquidem captivitati, inopiae, luctui, contemptui coniunctus est.

prevent you from being the best person to carry it out? If you love and serve your country intellectually, how could it not torment you to be unable to serve it physically? And wisdom itself makes the heartache worse, since you realize that the best laid plans are only as good as the best execution—and without a true patriot stepping up to act, they're worthless.

## ON SOCIAL CLASS

[18] I think that's enough about the stages of life; what should I say now about social stratification? Can I honestly deny that the upper, middle, and lower classes are equal in their misery?

Consider kings. Dionysius [*1 of Syracuse, tyrant from 405–367 BCE*] essentially proved how miserable and exposed to anxiety, dread, and plots they are when he had Damocles try out his "good fortune" for himself—by dangling a sword over his head. And no wonder, since kings endlessly face looming threats of war, devastation of their territories, massacres of their subjects, and annihilation of their cities. [19] When war *does* break out, the winner does always add a little glory or domain, but at such a cost and with such losses that it usually would've been better not to take up arms in the first place. If their army *does* get routed or some disaster strikes, moreover, it's the worst thing in the world, since it results in slavery, starvation, grief, and disgrace.

[20] Sed fac regem esse a bellorum impetu et a castrorum pulvere remotum, sua pacate possidentem, nullā hostium incursione vexatum: ¿num idcirco tutior, a miseriis securior? Quin immo, ut otium humana natura non fert, ipse sibi molestiam ac sollicitudinem exhibebit. Nam aut de augendis vectigalibus aut de producendis finibus deque urbibus ad imperium acquirendis aut de iungendis cum potentioribus propinquitatibus atque amicitiis cogitabit. Quae qui animo agitat, nec a molestiā liber est nec alios securos ac quietos esse sinit.

[21] De avaritiā, verò—maximā animorum peste—nolim hoc loco pluribus disputare: quae in deside atque otiosā mente quàm maxime exoritur, eaque erectiores animos et altiores dignitatis gradūs maxime sollicitat.

Huic generi, infimum hominum genus opponitur: quod ut nomine abiectissimum, sic re quoque omnibus calamitatibus atque angoribus est propositum. Huic inopia, fames, contumelia, iniuriae, tributorum solutio, militiae incommoda, misera denique omnia perferenda sunt, eoque miserius est quòd ceteris omnibus, quum adversā fortunā premuntur, permulta tamen suppetunt e quibus consolationem dolorisque levationem petunt. [22] At infimam plebem, natura ipsa—fatali quādam necessitate—tam abiecto tamque imo loco collocavit ut omnibus aerumnis subiecta,

[20] But imagine our king far removed from the melee of war and the dirty barracks. He's peacefully possessing his domains, with no trouble from enemy attacks. Is he any safer or less at risk of misery? No, far from it. He'll be his own source of stress and anxiety, since human nature cannot tolerate downtime. He'll be contemplating an increase in taxes, or plans to extend his borders and acquire cities for his domains, or to create ties of blood or friendship with mightier men. When your heart worries about those things, you have no peace yourself, and you allow no rest to others.

[21] And as for greed—the cancer of the soul—suffice it to say it almost invariably takes root in a lazy and idle mind, and that it's the great and powerful whose hearts are consumed by it the most.

The opposite of the upper class are the lower classes. As their name implies and their abject reality proves, they're vulnerable to every possible trauma and tragedy. They have to endure poverty, hunger, disrespect, aggressions, taxes, military disasters—basically, every conceivable misery. And what makes it even worse is that when something bad happens, everyone else at least has resources to cushion or help cope with the pain. [22] But from some fatal need, Nature itself has put the lower classes into *such* an abject position that under the weight of all

nullā prope modum ratione erigi aut sublevari possit.

Ne mediocris quidem hominum condicio miseriarum expers esse cognoscitur. Nam—inter summum et infimum interiecta—alteri paret, alterum patitur. Cui si imperare posset, certe longius a miseriā distaret. Sed quia neque dignitate praestat nec summos viribus adaequat, suo statu contenta esse cogitur. Itaque, multis in civitate perfungitur incommodis—non illis quidem parum rei publicae fructuosis, aut valde ad ferendum gravibus atque asperis, sed quae tamen animum sollicitent et humanas miserias augeant.

[23] Haec longiori oratione persequi, non est praesentis instituti; ante oculos omnia sunt et nobis praecipue re ipsā perspecta et cognita.

Nec verò alia est feminarum condicio; aut enim iisdem, aut parum certe diversis, et molestiis et angoribus vexantur; nam et iisdem morbis quibus viri, et iisdem animi perturbationibus mentisque erroribus, obiiciuntur. [24] Eoque miserior illarum status est quo mollior natura et,

those miseries, there's virtually no way for them to rise or lift themselves out.

The middle class is by no means misery-free either. It sits between the upper and the lower classes, and hence it's subservient to the one and stuck with the other. It'd certainly be less miserable if it could exploit the underclasses, but because it's little better than them in dignity, while it cannot match the resources of the elites, it's forced to be content with its status. Hence, it bears the brunt of society. True, those burdens do help run the country and they aren't excessively heavy or hard to bear. All the same, they cause anxiety and they increase human suffering.

[23] This is not the place to expand on these points; they're obvious to everyone, not least to me.


## ON WOMEN

It's no better for women. The problems and anxieties that torment them are the same as ours, or at least not much different. They're vulnerable to all the same traumas and heartaches and flights from reality that men are, [24] and in fact their condition

ad propulsanda incommoda calamitatesque perferendas, infirmior. Easdem quas viri ex parentum, fratrum, sororum, adfinium interitu molestias et dolores hauriunt; maritos saepe fatuos—parum de re domesticā sollicitos, pecuniam profundentes—nanciscuntur. [25] Ex quo, paupertas et luctus. Quibus malis, eo premuntur gravius quòd non—ut homines—indagare possunt quā maxime ratione medeantur incommodis rebusque suis consulant.

¡Quantum Tullia mea ex patris exsilio doloris, ¡quantum ex maritorum aerumnis et difficultatibus luctūs molestiaeque percepit! Et quamvis optanda etiam minime pauca in vitā viderit, malorum tamen paucorum sensus—vel doctissimis hominibus iudicantibus—ita acerbus est ut bonis vel plurimis et maximis aequetur, interdum etiam praeferatur. Permulta praeterea in hoc genere sunt quae reticere praestat quàm ēdere.

[26] Sed magna certe vel hoc uno nomine feminarum miseria est quòd, quamdiu vivunt, parēre semper coguntur: aut enim innuptae parentibus et adfinibus, aut

is even *more* miserable, in that they're naturally weaker and less capable of blocking out trauma and enduring tragedy. They suffer the same anxiety and pangs of grief that men do at the loss of parents, brothers, sisters, and relatives. They often get bum husbands whose stupidity, neglect, and blowing through money result in [25] poverty and grief. Even worse, the misery of their oppression is compounded because unlike men, women can't go out and look for the means to *repair* the damage and take financial control of their situation.

> Think of the *pain* my darling Tullia felt at her father's exile, all the grief and the problems that her husbands' screwups created! I *know* she saw her fair share of blessings in life. But, as the very wisest among us say, the taste of a few evils is so bitter that it can neutralize a world and lifetime of blessings—and sometimes even poison it. There's far more I'd like to say on this topic, but it's better kept to myself.

[26] All that said, there's one reason alone that explains why the misery of women is great: namely that all their lives long, *they're forever forced to obey*. They obey and owe subservience to their parents and relatives before they're married, or to their

nuptae maritis, parent et serviunt. Sic, quo minus liberae, eo magis miserae, nec umquam liberae nisi e vitā
profectae. Ergo, mortuae beatae censendae erunt. Nec
sane video quid aptius dici possit.

Sed ut ad nos ipsos redeamus: cui uxor contingit, is—
praeter communes omnium calamitates—praecipuo
etiam miseriae genere premitur, quòd non solum suis, sed
etiam domesticis uxoris et familiae molestiis curisque
vexatur; neque enim ab eā—quîcum artissimo matrimo-
nii vinculo conglutinatus est—aut mente aut cogitatione
seiunctus esse potest.

[27] Itaque, tot vexatus calamitatibus tantisque miseriis circumclusus, hominis animus ¿quid egregium aut ex-
imium suscipere aut cogitare potest? Mirum, ni sese
abiiciat ac, veluti desperatione perculsus, humi iaceat.

[28] Redeo igitur ad illud quod initio dixi, neminem esse,
qui spiritum ducat, non miserum, neminem vere felicem.
Parumque sapiunt ii qui **hominem luendorum scelerum**

husbands once they are. Hence, the less free they are, the more miserable they are; and since they're *never* free until they leave this life, it follows that only a dead woman must be accounted a happy woman. And I really don't see what more can be said.[11]

## BACK TO ME(N)

But to return to us, I say that beyond life's ordinary tragedies, a special kind of misery burdens a man who has the good fortune to be married, since his own problems are not his only source of torment. He shares in the worries and anxieties of his wife and family, since from her to whom he's united in matrimony — the strongest of all bonds — he cannot be divorced in mind or thought.

[27] And so, when a man's heart is so harassed by anxiety, so surrounded by misery, what great or outstanding project can he contemplate or take on? The *real* wonder is that he doesn't just sink down and lie on the floor in despair.

# Death Is Better than Life

## MAN WAS BORN TO ATONE FOR SINS

[28] And so I'm back to my original point [*in section 7*], that no one in existence is *not* miserable, no one is *truly* happy. **Man was born to atone for sins,**

**causā natum** felicem aut beatum audent nominare. [*V1*]
Nostra enim quae dicitur **"vita" mors est** [*V5*], nec umquam vivit animus nisi—compage solutus corporis—liber
aeternitate potiatur. [29] Itaque, mortem in beneficii loco
tributam a dis immortalibus iis quos maxime dilexerunt,
traditum est,

- ut quum—Herodoto auctore—Argia sacerdos, "quod
  optimum filiis" esset, a deā precata, eos repperit
  mortuos, mortem autem tamquam optimam illis esse
  concessam.
- Credamus sane Apollini Delphico, qui—exoratus a
  Trophonio et Agamede, a quibus templum magnifice
  Apollini exaedificatum Delphis erat—ut "quod esset
  optimum homini," tribueret; post diem tertium,
  exanimes sunt inventi. [30] Quo munere, indicavit
  deus—et deus is, cui divinationis partes a reliquis dis
  sunt relictae—mortem homini omnium rerum esse
  optimam.

Itaque, excutiatur iam et evellatur funditus falsa illa multorum opinio, malam esse mortem, quandoquidem vel deorum iudicio non modo mala non est, sed omnium rerum
optima et omnium munerum quae humano generi dari possunt, praestantissima. [31] Praeclare: nam et miseriarum
omnium quas viventes pertulimus, finis est in morte, et

and those who dare call him "happy" or "blessed" are naïve. Our **"life" is death,** and the heart or soul doesn't begin living until it's set free from the prison of the body, and gains eternity. [29] Hence, tradition has it, the immortal gods have granted death to those they love most as a benefit.

- For example, Herodotus says [*Histories 1.31*] the priestess of Argos prayed to the goddess for what was best for her sons—and found them dead, death being granted as if it were the best thing for them.
- And we should obviously believe Apollo of Delphi. After constructing a magnificent temple to Apollo at Delphi, Trophonius and Agamedes begged him to grant them what was best for a human being—and three days later, they were found lifeless. [30] By that gift, the god—the *same* god to whom all others had left the role of prophecy—indicated that for a human being, death is the best thing in the world.

So let's banish, let's *eradicate* the masses' false belief that death is bad, since by the gods' own decision not only is it *not* bad, it's the *best* of all things, and of all rewards that humankind can receive, the greatest. [31] And it clearly *is*, for death marks the end of all the miseries we endured in life, and an

vitatio futurarum in quas progredientes in vitā incurrunt.

Docemur enim exemplis, a propagatione vitae permultos optimos et fortissimos cives, incredibiles hausisse calamitates. "Immerentes," dixerit aliquis: "ergo, non sunt in miseriis ponendae. Nihil enim miserum quod non culpā contractum." De hoc aliàs viderimus, sed calamitates certe fuerunt—quarum etiam unica cogitatio, quae praetervolat et effugit, non modo sensus, qui corpori firmius inhaeret, acerbitatis habet plurimum.

[32] Ex quo, vere colligi potest sapienter fecisse Thraces, qui—si Herodoto credimus—nascentibus liberis lugere, morientibus laetari solebant. Exitum videlicet vitae ut miseriarum finem et quietis portum probabant, vitae initium ut ingressum ad molestias et dolores inviti videbant.

[33] Si, ergo, nascimur miseri, morimur beati, ¿quis in hanc lucem ēdi velit ut miseriis opprimatur? ¿quis non potius mori ut beatam vitam acquirat? et, si hoc nobismet ipsis ut optimum, vellemus, ¿cur liberis et adfinibus diversum? ¿An melius nobis quàm iis quos summe diligimus esse velimus, aut potius beate nobis, misere ipsis et infeliciter? Hoc, certe nullo modo. [34] Quamobrem, amanda mors semper omnibus, carissimis etiam optanda. Ac, si

escape from all the miseries that will be suffered by those who go on living.

Examples from history teach us that *many* excellent Romans suffered unimaginable tragedy by extending their lives. "Purely coincidental!" someone will say, "so don't call it 'misery,' because misery requires moral responsibility." Let's worry about that another time, because *tragedies* they surely were; a mere fleeting *thought* of them that flickers into mind is as agonizing as a lingering physical pain.

[32] And that suggests the Thracians were on to something, if it really was their custom (as Herodotus claims [5.4.2]) to grieve the births, and cheer the deaths, of children. They hailed life's exit as the end of miseries and a safe haven, and regarded its beginning, halfheartedly, as a portal to heartache and pain.[12]

[33] Therefore, if we're born miserable and we die happy, who would *want* to be born into this world? To drown in misery? Who *wouldn't* rather die if it meant obtaining a happy life? And if we did want that—what's "best" for ourselves—then why want any different for our children and relatives? Do we want better for ourselves than our loved ones? Or rather, happiness for us, but heartache and misery for them? Of course not. [34] It follows, then, that everyone should *love* death, always, and

quibus mori praestat quàm vivere, iis praecipue, quos et acta cum virtute vita claros effecit, et mors—satis diuturnā vitā perfunctos—molestiā adficere non potest.

[35] Nasci, verò—non intellego quibus expediat. Nam in aerumnas miseriasque ingredientes, ¿quid gratum, quid hilare aspicimus? ¿Quare potius non offendimur? quod primus ille nascentium infantium vagitus et eiulatus satis declarat. Tributus enim est ab optimā parente naturā, quae nihil inane solet efferre ac potius iis rebus quas efficit, admiranda semper ēdit vel pietatis vel iustitiae vel prudentiae documenta. [36] Ex quo, intellegi licet **non nasci longe optimum esse nec in hos scopulos incidere vitae, proximum autem, si natus sis, quàm primum mori et tamquam ex incendio effugere <violentiam>** [*supplied by Lactantius*] **fortunae.** [*V9*]

Sileni quae fertur fabula—si gravioribus ludicra interdum admiscere liceat—idem certe confirmat: qui captus a Midā, missionem doctrinā redemit. Docuit autem regem numquam nasci optimum esse, sed celeritatem mortis proxime accedere. Idemque Euripidis testimonio, poetae sapientissimi, comprobatur. [37] Sed Crantor noster patri—fili mortem aegerrime ferenti—responsum ait datum esse

even wish for it for their dearest. And if there's *any-one* for whom dying is better than living, it's undoubtedly those who have lived lives of greatness and become eminent for it, and hence, having had a good run, can die without regret.

## IT'S BEST TO NEVER BE BORN

[35] Being *born*, though—I don't get who it's good for. Where's the evidence of happiness or joy in us entering a world of misery? Isn't it rather that we're outraged, as the screaming and crying of newborn babies implies? Yes, because those screams are a gift of Mother Nature's brilliance. She does nothing in vain, and in fact is always leaving proof of the love, justice, or design behind her creations.[13] It's fascinating, [36] and it shows why **not being born and hence hurled against life's rocks is clearly the best option. Second best, if you do get born, is to die and flee the violence of Fortune as fast as you'd run from a burning building.**

If adding folklore to serious philosophy is occasionally okay, then "The Story of Silenus" confirms it. Imprisoned by Midas, Silenus won his freedom by teaching the king that never being born is best, while dying soon comes second. A passage of Euripides, wisest of poets, makes the same point.[14] [37] Meanwhile Crantor, our authority [*section 7*], says a father shattered by his son's death received this answer

in psychomantio, filio suo bene beateque esse utiliusque
futurum fuisse si etiam pater pari ratione fatis concessisset.

Quamobrem,

- si dolorum finem mors adfert,
- si securioris et melioris initium vitae,
- si futura mala avertit,
- si medetur praesentibus,
- si nos ex plurimis vel morborum vel molestiarum vel
  acerbitatum periculis educit,

¿cur eam tanto opere accusare aut dolorem ex eā derivare
velimus, ex qua potius consolationem ac laetitiam haurire
fas esset?

Nisi si quod mortem subsequitur, nos fortasse solicitos habet. [38] De quo libet pauca dicere, ne hic unus ad
molestiam doloremque alendum angulus relinquatur, qui
profectò insipientibus obiiciendus non est nec in tanto argumentorum acervo quibus mortem ipsam nobis obstringere conamur, committendum ut hoc uno nomine
minus nobis debere videatur.

Et quamquam haec futuri post mortem temporis cura
hominis propria non sit, sed dis immortalibus potius relinquenda, quorum nos vel liberalitati vel sapientiae permittere fas piumque esset—qui enim nascentium curam

at a séance: "Your son is happy and at peace, and it would do you good to meet the same fate."

Therefore, if death:

- brings an end to pain,
- leads to the beginning of a more secure and better life,
- prevents future evils,
- heals present ones, and
- delivers us from countless threats of trauma, regret, and heartache,

Then why should we rage against death so angrily? Why blame pain on what *should* by rights be a source of joy and comfort?

All I can think is, it's what comes *after* death that worries us. [38] I want to say something about that, to make sure this one area doesn't get left for people's anxieties to feed on. It cannot and must not be abandoned to fools, and after all the arguments I'm marshalling to vouch for death, I cannot allow death this one pretext to feel any less indebted to me.

## WHAT HAPPENS AFTER DEATH

I know the time after death is not properly man's concern, that it belongs to the immortal gods whose generosity and wisdom we're duty-bound to trust. I mean, if they agree to take charge of us at birth,

suscipiunt, qui viventes protegunt, alunt, tuentur, fovent, ¿cur morientes deserant?—

tamen aliquid etiam modeste de iis exquirere non est inutile. Necesse est autem sit alterum de duobus, ut:

- aut sensūs penitus omnes mors auferat,
- aut in alium quendam locum ex his locis morte migretur.

[39] Quod si morte sensus exstinguitur, obitusque noster ei somno similis est qui nonnumquam etiam sine visis somniorum placatissimam quietem adfert, ¡quid lucri est emori! aut ¡¿quod omnino tempus reperiri potest quod ei tempori anteponatur cui similis futura est perpetuitas omnis consequentis aetatis?!

Sin migrationem malimus esse mortem in eas oras quas e vitā profecti incolunt, ¿quid optabilius quàm ad eos proficisci quos mortuos vivens dilexeris, et cum iis perpetuā vitā perfrui qui, ut nos in laude viveremus et libenter moreremur, suis et praeceptis et exemplis tanto opere laborarunt? [40] Mihi certe nihil videtur evenire posse gratius quàm—si mors aditum ad alia loca patefaciat—ad eos venire et cum iis esse quos et maxime dilexi et numquam non diligere ac laudare possum. Ad meos autem et adfines et amicos ut pervenero, ¡quanto opere laetabor! ¿Quae

and they protect, nourish, watch over, and support us in life, then why should they abandon us at the hour of death?

Still, there's value in devoting at least a little attention to it, since it must entail one of these two scenarios:

- Death either obliterates all consciousness, or
- It transports us to some other place.

[39] If death extinguishes consciousness, if our passing is like the rare, dreamless sleep that brings complete and total relaxation, then—well, what a *deal* dying is! What time could you possibly prefer to *that* time—which will continue in like fashion throughout the endless eons that follow?

Alternatively, if we'd rather death be a moving on to the regions where the departed dwell, then what could be more enviable than reuniting in death with those you loved in life? Than enjoying eternal life with those whose teachings and examples so influenced us to live honorably and to die without regrets? [40] I can't imagine anything more wonderful than having death open up a portal to that other place, and finding and being with those I loved most, people I could never stop loving and praising. And how I'll *rejoice* when I reach my

iucundior collocutio, ¿qui suavior vel congressus vel complexus? ¡O

"vitam" vere "vitalem"

ut ait Ennius—omnibus bonis ac gaudiis circumfluentem—sed ¡beatam etiam mortem, quae ad beatissimam vitam aditum aperiat!

Me quidem, etsi dolore vehementer perculsum et adflictum, his tamen monitis et praeceptis non mediocriter adlevari sentio. [41] Itaque, neminem puto fore quem non rationes a nobis tam studiose e sapientium libris collectae iuvent ac delectent, eoque magis, quo leviores erunt aliorum dolores quàm hic, quo nos tanto opere vexati sumus.

> Nam si amor, si pietas filiae, si virtus, si gravitas, si constantia, si cetera quae vix in feminis spectari—nedum requiri—solent, consideranda sint, tantā factā iacturā gravissime dolere debuimus.

Sed vincat dolorem consolatio; nec iam quid amiserimus, sed quatenus mortalem filiam lugere deceat,

relatives and friends! Can you imagine any conversation more wonderful, any sweeter reunion or embrace? Oh, truly a

"life worth living,"

as Ennius says, filled with every joy and good! But also, what a blessing *death* is, if it opens the door to the happiest life!

The grief consuming me is truly staggering, but I for one *do* feel genuinely uplifted by these thoughts and considerations. [41] And it makes me think there's no one who *won't* find some relief or delight in the reflections I've so carefully collected from the books of experts [*cf. section 4*]. Indeed, to the extent that others' heartaches prove less severe than my own agony, I suspect it will help them all the more.

I mean, if we're to consider a daughter's love and devotion, her greatness, dignity, strength and all the other qualities you scarcely see, much less *look* for in a woman, then it was inevitable that grief at such a loss would shatter me.

But consolation *must* prevail over grief. I have to stop focusing on what I've lost and start focusing on how far I should mourn a daughter who was

cogitemus. Hoc, nos in maerore nostro, quod certe fortis est aegroti: non solum accipere, sed etiam exquirere medicinam.

[42] At siquis erit quem dolor a ratione averterit, cui non satis firma videantur ea quae iam dicta sunt, is:

- se hominem esse meminerit;
- nihil, autem, humanius esse morte; ut, si mors ab ipso divelli atque auferri posset, dis propior habendus esset quàm hominibus, nec omni ex parte hominis nomen ipsi congrueret, quia communi et praecipuā hominis condicione non uteretur;
- praeterea, lacrimis nihil profici; quae, si quid adiumenti adferre possent, non solum effundendae sed studiose conquirendae, viderentur;

- [43] denique, non solum iniuste sed etiam turpissime agere, qui immodice doleat; turpitudo enim peior est dolore, siquidem dolor homini a naturā insitus est nihilque habet infamiae. Turpitudo, autem, idcirco vituperanda quòd aliquid semper indecorum continet, culpā contractum.

only mortal. And in doing that, I'm doing in my grief what tough people do when they get sick: they don't just accept a remedy, they go out and find one.

## Death Is Part of the Human Condition

[42] Still, if grief is clouding anyone's judgment and they decide that what I've said so far isn't solid or reliable enough, then remember:

- You're human.
- Nothing is more human than death. If death could be ripped out of you and spirited away, you'd be more god than human. The name "human" wouldn't really fit you, since you'd be skipping the most universal and characteristically human experience.
- Tears achieve nothing. If they did, you'd not only want to shed them copiously, you'd want to force them out zealously.
- [43] If you grieve excessively, you're not just misguided, you're also disgracing yourself. That's because disgrace is worse than grief, inasmuch as grief is a natural human instinct and there's nothing shameful about it; whereas disgrace should be criticized precisely because it always entails some stain of guilt.

At omnis immodicus dolor turpis est et a viro alienus, quandoquidem ut immodice praeterque rationem doleas, sponte efficis. Ex quo, culpa exoritur; quae homini maxime fugienda vitandaque est, ne cogitationibus mollissimis—quales interdum perdite amantes suscipere solent—nimium perturbemur et effeminemur. [44] Quin potius, nos ad Homerica praecepta referamus:

> ♫*Corde, age, sis firmo, nec te submitte dolori;*
> *namque aliquid gravius peiusque aliquando tulisti.*♫

Nemo, videlicet, suorum funera experitur cui non adversa multa antea contigerint: ita variis omni ex parte incommodis, humana natura concluditur. ¿Cur, igitur, graviora vel certe aeque gravia fortiter passus—quum maxime occalluisse et ad dolorem novum obduruisse deberet—despondeat animum seque maerori tradat?

Quod etiam iniustum esse, paulo ante dicebamus. Natura enim usuram nobis vitae dedit, tamquam pecuniae, nullā praefinitā die. Quod si quum libet sua repetit, eā

# HOW TO GRIEVE

## EXCESSIVE GRIEF IS DISGRACEFUL
## AND MISGUIDED

All excessive grief is disgraceful and unnatural because grieving excessively and unreasonably is a conscious *choice*. It engenders a weakness that men must shun and abhor, lest we become overwrought and effeminate from the kind of soft and sappy thoughts lovers are always abandoning themselves to. [44] No, we do better to remember the Homeric rule [*Odyssey 20.18*]:

> ♪*Come on, get tough, and harden your heart!*
> *Don't surrender to grieving.*
> *You've already endured in the past far worse and*
> *far graver.*♪

Human nature is so inescapably fraught with tragedy that no one, obviously, attends a loved one's funeral without having suffered many setbacks already. So, if you've already powered through worse or at least as bad—where the pain you had to steel yourself for was something new—then why should you lose all hope and surrender to depression now?

I was just saying how that's also misguided [*section 43, 4*]. You see, Nature gave us life on loan, like money, with no fixed maturity date. If she comes

condicione commodatā ut restituenda sint, ¿cur accusatur? ¿aut cur non potius naturae gratias agis quòd, quum citius potuisset, tardius repetierit, quàm quòd aliquando repetierit, iniustā querelā insequeris? [45] Certum est enim non habitandi locum, sed commorandi deversorium nobis esse concessum; e quo quum migramus, alacres tamquam ex hospitio miseriarum atque incommodorum plenissimo egredi debemus ac laetissimo animo ad futuram vitam tamquam ad patriam evolare. Quod sapientes re ipsā praestitisse memorantur.

Profectò enim, siquid est quod morientes perturbet aut morientium adfines habeat sollicitos, id totum:

[1] aut ex falsā quadam opinione oritur, quòd vitae huius usum nimis utilem ac iucundum arbitremur,
[2] aut ex nimio in nosmet ipsos amore caritateque provenit.

Sed opinionem illam, quam rationes adeo firmae convellunt, libenter deponere debemus; ab hoc verò amore nimio, tanto libentius abhorrere quanto indecentius est vitae munere perfunctos

- velle etiam in vitā—dis invitis—commorari,
- communemque omnium qui ante nos e vitā discesserunt, condicionem recusare;

to collect what's hers when the whim takes her—
*and* she lent it on condition that it be returned—
then why criticize her? Why not instead *thank*
Nature for coming later rather than sooner, instead
of ranting that she's finally come at all? [45] We
*know* we're granted a hotel room, not a permanent
residence. When we check out, we should go *cheerfully*, like we're leaving a horrible, crummy hostel.
We should soar with the greatest optimism to our
future life, like we're heading home—as *true* sages,
we're told, have actually done.

You see, if anything distresses the dying and
leaves their relatives upset, it surely results from
either:

[*1*] the misguided belief that this life is better and
more joyous than it is, or
[*2*] our selfishness and narcissism.

But solid arguments annihilate [*1*] and we should
abandon it, whereas we ought to abhor [*2*] as fully
as we recognize how unseemly it is, once our careers
in life are over, to:

• try to stay on despite the gods' will,
• refuse the universal terms imposed on all who left
before us, and

- demum, tantā esse mollitie tantāque impudentiā ut ne in morte quidem confirmemur ac resipiscamus.

[46] Quod si nostrorum mortem dolemus, cogitemus:

- aliquando moriendum ipsis fuisse;
- mortem autem incertam esse, nec in hominis arbitrio positam, sed e deorum voluntate pendēre;
- quos verò lugemus, eos quoque suorum mortem vidisse patienterque tulisse, ideoque suo exemplo quid nos facere velint, praecipere;
- denique, id quod ad consolandum maximum ac firmissimum est, non eos nobis penitus ereptos esse nec prorsus amissos, sed ad praefinitum tempus a nostris oculis nostrāque consuetudine remotos.

[47] Itaque, quum ad eum vitae terminum quem natura praescripsit nos quoque pervenerimus, statim eorum consuetudinem regustabimus, et ad suavissimam vel consuetudinem vel convictum redibimus.

Mortem suis acerbam amaramque in moriendo esse, nonnulli existimant, atque ideo fortasse perturbantur.

- be so worthless and weak that we don't get tough and pull it together even in our final moments.

[46] If it's the death of our loved ones that's tormenting us, then let's reflect that:

- They had to die someday.
- Death is uncertain and not up to man; it depends on the will of the gods.
- Those we're mourning watched their *own* loved ones die, and they endured it with forbearing. Hence, they teach us by example the behavior they'd have us model.
- Finally—to drive home the most comforting point—*they aren't lost or gone forever. They've just been taken somewhere we can't see or talk to them a while.*

[47] That means that when we too reach the end of life that Nature has prescribed, we'll instantly taste the pleasure of their company again. We'll resume our happy times—or reunite.

## DYING IS NOT PAINFUL

Some believe their loved ones' death is painful and the process agonizing, and that may be what upsets them.

Quod me quidem—sublatis gravioribus dolendi causis quas iam superiori disputatione reiecimus—minime angit. Ipse enim discessus animi a corpore vel cum nullo vel certe cum modico dolore fit, et interdum sine sensu; nonnumquam etiam, si recte sapimus, cum voluptate. [48] Sed quidquid sit, totum hoc ita leve est qualia sunt ea quae puncto temporis fiunt.

Nec, si mors paulo longior alicui contingat, desperandum est de deorum naturaeque benignitate quin eo quoque tempore properantem e vitā discedere foveant atque adlevent. Cuius rei in morientibus saepissime signa minime dubia cernuntur; quum—velut e somno exciti—quo tempore extremum spiritum edituri sunt, ita gaudentes et alacres aspiciunt ut libentissime iudices e vitā proficisci.

[49] Quamobrem, ne haec quidem ullam aequam doloris adferre causam possunt—qui, certe, comprimendus ac minuendus est, quòd etiam si nolis, tempore tamen ipso extenuatur et evanescit: non quòd minuendi doloris vis in ipsā die posita sit, sed quòd usus ipse cogitatioque diuturni temporis doceat nihil esse in morte mali, ideoque leviter et patienter ferendam.

[50] Sed turpe stultumque est homini tantā tamque variā rerum cognitione instructo non a se ipso

Well, having eliminated the more important reasons for grieving already [*sections 28–46*], I'm not
worried about that at all. You see, the departure of the
soul from the body occurs without any or only mod-
erate pain. Sometimes there's no feeling at all, and occasionally—if we're not mistaken—it's even pleasur-
able. [48] Whichever it is, though, the whole thing's as
minor as anything that's over with in a second.

If death *does* take some a little longer, we mustn't
fail to trust that the goodness of the gods and of
Nature are continuing to provide nurture and comfort in their struggle to die. We often see unmistak-
able signs of that in the dying. The moment they're
about to breathe their last, they gaze up, like people
waking up from sleep, so happy and so bright that
you'd swear they're enjoying leaving life.

[49] Hence, even that concern can't really justify
grief. No: you have to *repress* grief, *overcome* it—
because in time, it does thin out and disappear, even
if you'd rather it not. It's not that time itself possesses the power to overcome grief; it's simply that
habit and daily reflection teach us that there's
nothing bad about death, and hence we should endure it lightly and patiently.

[50] When a man's seen so much, though,
it's shameful and stupid to wait for habit and
reflection to supply remedies for his grief

potius mature, quàm serò ab usu et cogitatione, doloris remedia exspectare.

Quae tam firma sunt ut neminem fore putem quem non
vehementer non iuvent solùm, sed etiam permoveant.

Mihi, verò, eo magis necessaria fuerunt quo turpius
visum esset, me—qui ceteros constantissime consolatus
essem—in meo dolore iacēre; voxque illa exaudiri, et fortasse non immeritò, potuisset:

♫ ¿Hicine ille Cicero . . .
*cuius ob os Graii ora obvertebant sua?* ♫

Sed nos philosophia adversùs omnes vel temporum vel
fortunae vel naturae insidias munivit; quae ita fortis est
ut nullius iniuriae impetum extimescat, ita lenis et suavis
ut omnes acerbitates facile mitiget ac molliat, ita demum
utilis et fructuosa ut totam se ad humanas utilitates liber-
alissime porrigat atque explicet.

[51] Nec verò secus debet; quae enim humanarum
miseriarum cumulum optime norit et acutissime perspi-
ciat, si eas patiatur manare longius neque homini maerore

on their own time. No, the *worldly* man should look straight to *himself* for them [*cf. section 41*].

## THE PSYCHOTHERAPEUTIC VALUE OF PHILOSOPHY

The foregoing arguments [*sections 42–49*] are so solid and reliable that everyone will, I believe, find them not just enormously helpful, but persuasive.

Moreover, I needed them *myself*, given the shame I felt that *I* — always a staunch consoler of others — was paralyzed with grief. I knew I'd hear the taunt, and perhaps with justice,

♫*Is* this *the selfsame Cicero whose eloquence Greek gazes turned to meet?!?*♫

What's fortified me against every pitfall of circumstance and fortune and nature, though, is philosophy. Philosophy is so mighty that she cowers before no assault; so sweet and gentle that she soothes and eases every heartache; and so generous and wonderful that she lends and extends her whole self to human progress.

[51] And that's as it should be. I mean, Philosophy knows mankind's accumulated miseries intimately and diagnoses them precisely. If she let them fester when a man's wracked with grief, if she were

confecto consilio praesidioque suo praestò sit, ¿quid illo miserius? ¿quid vitā nostrā laboriosius aut taetrius? ¿Aut quid prodesset aspectum a naturā ad supera erectum accepisse, ut caelum contemplari, ut deorum maiestatem cogitare, aut a dis immortalibus mentem et rationem ut utilia cognoscere, honesta a turpibus secernere, aequa amplecti, ab iniquis abstinere possemus, voce denique ipsā et oratione frui—quae nullis animantibus concessa est, quaque ceteris omnibus quae sub caelo sunt viventium naturis antecellimus? Inania haec videri possent, si tam multis ex adverso miseriis oppressa hominis natura neque se ad caelestia erigere nec tantis bonis, quibus maiora nulla esse potuerunt, uti posset.

[52] Sed profectò ut contra serpentium virus pharmacorum genera multa, contra inopiae calamitatem sollertia et industria, contra turpitudinis voluptatem pudor et verecundia, sic contra doloris morsum philosophia nobis data est deorum immortalium concessu atque munere. Quam ut nemo satis pro dignitate laudare queat, sic quàm plurimi mentis tranquillitatem, animi moderationem, in voluptates imperium, in acerba omnia summam quandam vim ac fortitudinem illi uni acceptam referant, necesse est. Neque nos aut in exilio patientes aut in honorum cursu temperantes fuissemus aut nunc in tanto maerore sapienter et fortiter versaremur, nisi tuo, philosophia— optima rerum humanarum moderatrix—beneficio.

unavailable as counselor and support, what could you pity more? Could any burden, any horror be worse than life itself? What good would Nature's privilege to us be of having faces lifted up to contemplate the heavens, to ponder the gods' majesty? Or the immortal gods giving us rational minds to learn useful skills, distinguish good from bad, embrace justice, to refrain from evil? Or indeed, language itself, a concession no other creature enjoys, and which makes us naturally superior to every other animal under heaven? With human nature so battered and oppressed by miseries, these gifts could all seem pointless if human nature had no hope of elevating itself toward heaven or of putting such perfect blessings to use.

[52] But we *do!* Because just as we have various antidotes to counteract snakes' venom, and a strong work ethic to counteract gripping poverty, and self-respect to counteract base pleasures, so *Philosophy* is the immortal gods' gift to us to counteract gnawing grief. No one can praise Philosophy as she deserves, but we must all at least thank her, and her alone, for our gifts of inner peace, self-control, impulse control, and our awesome strength and fortitude in the face of bitter experience. Without *your* beneficence, Philosophy, I never could've endured exile, checked my ambitions, or have the wisdom and strength now to hold up in my grief. For human affairs, you are the finest of guides.

[53] Tu, verò, felix et beata, Tullia mea—si quis tibi in morte sensus est—quae tot tantisque miseriis quibus proposita fuisses in vitā, unā morte perfuncta es, a praesentibus malis expedita, ab impendentibus erepta et in tuto ac tranquillo quietis portu collocata. Meritò tibi mortem iucundam fuisse putem, quum vel ea bona quibus viventi frui licuit, animo reputas, vel mala quae moriens vitasti, mente ac cogitatione complecteris.

[54] Ego autem, quum te felicem iudicem ac, si dicere liceat, paene oculis cernam, ¿cur tuā morte excrucier? Potius laetabor, ac tibi tamquam de re optatissimā gratulabor. Cui nisi molestum est me iam aetate confectum in tam perturbatā re publicā tamque misero vitae genere reliquisse, ¿quid iam grave aut acerbum esse possit?

[55] Sed hoc quoque ratione ipsā levius aliquanto efficitur, neque tu nunc quid me perferre necesse sit, sed quàm non multo post tecum iisdem bonis usurus sim, debes cogitare. Nihil enim accidere valde grave potest iis qui spe iam propinquā futuri boni recreantur et aluntur.

**Sed nescio qui nos teneat error aut miserabilis ignoratio veri.** [V2] Non enim tanto opere bonis delectamur quàm malis adfligimur. Ex quo, fit ut haec

# HOW TO GRIEVE

## TO TULLIA IN HEAVEN

[53] As for *you*, my precious Tullia—if you can hear me in death—you're happy. By dying once, you put an end to all the unhappiness you faced in life. You're freed from your problems, spared the ones looming, and sheltered now, safe and secure. I can readily believe you found death pleasant, since you're either remembering the good parts of life or appreciating the misery you evaded by dying.

[54] And since I'm deciding *you*'re happy—can almost (if I can say it) *see* it—why should your death torment *me*? I'll *rejoice* instead, and congratulate you like you've gotten your fondest wish. And unless you're upset at leaving *me* behind—wracked with old age, the country polarized, eking out life—what could trouble or pain you now?

[55] But reason helps a bit with that, too. Your job now isn't to worry about me, but to focus on how I'll soon be enjoying those same blessings with you. You see, no misfortune is too hard to bear when you nurture realistic hopes of a good thing coming.

## WE LIVE IN DENIAL

The problem is, **I don't understand what mistake—or sad denial of reality—has gotten hold of us.** Good things don't make us as happy as bad things make us miserable, so we end up multiplying the

etiam nolentes augeamus; bona autem, quae fruendo, cogitando, gaudendo maiora efficere expediret, etiam deteramus; quod certe minime oporteret. Nam, si serriò disputare volumus,

- ¿cur dolores resque adversas refugiamus, quae fortitudinem in nobis gignunt et efficiunt? [56] Quae si nulla essent, nulla profectò fortitudo agnosceretur.
- ¿Cur mortem horreamus, quae adsiduā sui memoriā nos ut meliores simus admonet? nec patitur ad ea nos animum adiungere quae aliquam nomini nostro vel intemperantiae vel iniustitiae notam possint inurere.
- Bona, verò, et ea quae probantur in vulgus, ¿cur tanto opere appetamus? quae consecuti, molliores plerùmque ac deteriores evadimus. [57] Itaque, his voluptatum lenociniis obruimur, ut discessum ex hāc vitā impendēre vix aliquando recordemur.

Sapienter philosophorum princeps et magister Plato:

"Quae sensus appetit aut timet, nihil aliud esse quàm somnia; itaque, penitus contemnenda esse. Mala verò ut vitentur, ad aeterna properandum; quo nisi confugias, vitari numquam posse."

latter even despite ourselves. Meanwhile, we actually *waste* the blessings we *ought* to increase by using, appreciating, and enjoying them. It makes no sense. If we actually think about it,

- Why run from pain and adversity? They breed fortitude in us, and [56] without them we'd never know what it means to be mentally tough.
- Why flinch at death? Its steady drumbeat admonishes us to better ourselves. It stops us from engaging in activities that could earn us a reputation for intemperance or injustice.
- Conversely, why crave material things and the junk the masses love? Once we have them, we become soft, weak, [57] and so overwhelmed by those seductions that we barely remember it's all coming to an end someday.

The grand master of philosophers, Plato, put it wisely:

"The objects that our senses desire or fear are nothing but dreams, and hence should be utterly despised. To actually avoid evil, you must resort to eternity; without seeking refuge there, avoiding it is impossible."[15]

At ad aeterna ne properari quidem potest nisi morte ian-
itore ac duce.

[58] ¿Quorsum haec? ut intellegamus non modo a dolore vacuam, quietam, opportunam, bonam denique esse
mortem, sed etiam summorum atque immortalium bonorum liberalem ac beneficam ministram.

Itaque, Cato sic e vitā discessit ut laetaretur causam se
nactum esse moriendi. Iam nemini dubium esse potest
quin vir prudentissimus, si suā morte laetabatur, mortem
etiam optimam esse agnosceret. [59] Certe enim in re suā,
quae praesertim sensu percipiatur, nemo fallitur.

Quod comprobare possum Artabani, Xerxis patrui,
viri sapientissimi, testimonio. De quo est apud Herodo-
tum, quum Xerxes exercitūs sui copias paene innumera-
biles ante se in aciem instructas intuens collacrimatus
esset neminem ex tot milibus ad centum annos supers-
titem futurum, illum Xerxi respondisse:

"At tam multa sunt tamque misera quae viventes
perferunt, ut nemo sit quin mori saepissime
cupiat, quum incidentes calamitates et morbi
vitam adeo perturbent sollicitamque habeant ut

Even "resorting" to eternity is impossible, however, without death as our doorman and guide!

[58] What's my point? It's this: death isn't just painless, peaceful, timely, and in short, a blessing. It's also the generous and beneficial *agent* of supreme and eternal blessings.

### PREMATURE DEATH IS BEST

This explains why Cato [*the Younger*] left this world suggesting he was excited to have gotten a reason to die. Now, it's obvious that if a man as wise and disciplined as Cato congratulated himself on his death, he also recognized that death is the greatest good, [59] because no one misjudges their own interests, especially tangible interests.

I can prove it by a statement of Artabanus, uncle of Xerxes and a man of great wisdom. According to Herodotus [*Histories* 7.46], when Xerxes surveyed his army's nearly infinite troops arrayed before him, he wept at the thought that of so many soldiers, in a hundred years not one would be alive. Artabanus replied,

> "Yes, but life's sufferings are so many and so intense that there isn't one who hasn't repeatedly *wished* to die, any time horrible accidents or illness make life so taxing and stressful that it

longissima videatur. [60] Itaque, mortem perfugium esse aerumnosae vitae, dubitare nemo potest."

Nec his contentus, addit etiam illud:

"Deos immortales, quum hominum vitam, quae adeo misera sit, multis bonorum integumentis velarunt et operuerunt, fecisse quodam modo invidentius, ne mortis suavitatem, quanta est, omni ex parte degustaremus."

Amphiaraum fabulae narrant Iovi atque Apollini fuisse carissimum, neque tamen illum senium attigisse. [61] Ex quo, ¿quid aliud coniici potest quàm mortis celeritatem divinum munus et lucrum esse maximum? Itaque, scitum est illud comicum—

♫*Nam quem tuetur atque diligit deus,*
*iuvenis supremum mortis intrat limitem.*♫

—neminem enim quem dilexerint di patiuntur esse miserum. Quare, vitam eis miseriarum plenam adimant necesse est.

[62] ¿Quid autem contingere homini tam gratum potest quod eum magno opere in vitā retineat?

seems too long. [60] Hence, death is undeniably a refuge from an unbearable life."

And not stopping there, he added,

> "The life of man is so horrible that when the immortal gods dressed it up in the trappings of happiness, they did so a bit grudgingly, to keep us from tasting the full sweetness of death."

Mythology tells us Jupiter and Apollo loved Amphiaraus dearly—and yet he did not reach old age. [61] The inescapable conclusion, therefore, is that a *speedy* death is a gift of the gods and an enormous blessing. That quotation from comedy gets it exactly:

> ♫*The man God loves and lovingly protects,*
> *steps through death's final portal in his teens.*♫

That's because the gods don't let anyone they love be miserable, and so they *have* to take a life filled with miseries away from them.

## CAREER SUCCESS IS AN ILLUSION

[62] What success in life can prove so satisfying that it makes you determined to live?

- Voluptas, credo, quam ex alicuius sive artis sive doctrinae tractatione percipit. At doctrina aemulationem, omnium rerum molestissimam, si quaeris, etiam dolorem parit. Non tam enim delectamur aliquid discentes quàm angimur, multo plura ac maiora quae scire vellemus penitus ignorantes.

- Artes, verò, quas tenuiores tractant, ¿quid habent voluptatis aut quid non potius molestiarum et maeroris? ¡Quanta inter eos qui illas exercent perfidia, quantum odium, quanta invidia! aut ¿quis est suā sorte contentus et non alienae sive industriae sive fortunae aemulator, osor, detractor?

- [63] Sin civilem vitam quisquam appetit et in rei publicae luce vivere pulchrum putat, is se exiguā ac paene nullā honoris specie magnas comparare calamitates certò sciat! ¿Quotus enim quisque est cui non publica administratio vel maeroris vel iacturae tantum attulerit quantum verbis explicare vix queat?

Ac, si de toto vitae cursu iudicare vere volumus, exitum videamus. ¿Ubi optimi rei publicae administratores, seu verius parentes, Miltiades, Ephialtes, Cimo, Themistocles, Aristides? ¡Quantum illis fides, caritas, integritas, constantia peperit miseriae! ut non modo honoribus,

- The satisfaction of mastering some art or body of knowledge? Maybe, but if you look around, expertise breeds jealousy, with all its exasperations—and grief, too, since learning something is less fulfilling than anxiety-inducing, in making us ignore many other more important things we'd like to know.

- Pursuit of the fine arts, perhaps? But where's the joy—or rather, absence of heartache—in *that*? Look at the backstabbing, the hatred, the *jealousy* among their practitioners! Are *any* of them content with their career? Do any *not* rival, hate on, or criticize others' hard work or luck?!

- [63] If you're drawn to public life and want to bask in politics, make no mistake: in exchange for—at best—token recognitions, you're setting yourself up for major problems. I mean, does anyone *not* find inexpressible heartache and loss in public administration?

If we want an *accurate* view of an entire career, we should look at its *end*. Miltiades, Ephialtes, Cimon, Themistocles, and Aristides, Greece's greatest administrators—or rather, statesmen: where did *they* end up? Loyalty, dedication, integrity, and commitment brought them nothing but misery. They were stripped of honors, respect, power, even shipped

dignitate, auctoritate spoliarit, sed etiam in exsilium mise-
rit. Quod contra oportebat, viros optimos patriaeque
amantissimos honore adfici, in oculis ferri.

Scipio Africanus apud nostros optimam causam am-
plexus, paucorum immoderatae libidini repugnans, mane
mortuus in lecto est inventus, nec abfuit suspicio quin ab
uxore, quae Gracchorum soror fuit, interfectores essent
immissi.

[64] Metello autem Numidico, homine omnium clar-
issimo ac praestantissimo, ¿quid miserius? qui, ne in
legem perniciosam iuraret, in exsilium abire sit coactus.
Fateor profectò inter omnia exsilii genera atque omnes
miseriarum causas maxime honestam Numidici fuisse
condicionem, cui probitas, integritas, in patriam caritas
calamitatis causam attulerit, sed tamen fatendum est
gravissimam fuisse calamitatem pelli patriā, avelli a suis,
bonorum direptionem, liberorum sive maestitiam sive
aerumnam videre.

[65] M. Regulum, C. Marium, L. Brutum ob liberan-
dam patriam interfectum praetereo; nolim in iis com-
memorandis nimius videri, quorum exitūs nemo est quin
ex libris, imaginibus, famā denique vulgari iam didicerit.

off into exile! It should've been the opposite, with those incredible patriots honored and adored.

Among us Romans, Scipio Aemilianus [*Consul 147 and 134 BCE*] embraced the best cause, fought the outrageous greed of the few, and was found dead in bed one morning—with some even suspecting that his wife, a sister of the Gracchi brothers, had let the killers in.

[64] Metellus Numidicus [*Consul 109 BCE*] was a truly outstanding man, and what could be worse than *his* fate? To avoid swearing allegiance to a pernicious law, he was forced into exile. I grant that of all possible kinds of exile and causes of misery, Metellus's was the most honorable, in that his goodness, integrity, and patriotism were the cause of his suffering. That said, being ordered out of your homeland, torn from your loved ones, seeing your property confiscated, and watching the sobbing and suffering of your children: *those* were undeniably horrors beyond imagining.

[65] I'll pass over Regulus, Marius, and Brutus, who was killed for liberating our country. There's no point in me recounting the fate of men already known to everyone from books, portraits, and oral tradition.

Quae quum multa maximeque gravia sint, gravissimum tamen illud debet videri, quod homine ambitionis vinculis irretito quique e popularibus suffragiis totus pendeat, nihil usquam infelicius reperiri potest. ¡Quantus in eo timor, quanta dubitatio, quantus conatus, quanta sollicitudo! ut nullam illi a molestiā vacuam esse horam non immeritò suspicari possimus. Nam si servientis ea est condicio ut ex eius, cui servit, moribus, voluntate, ingenio propriam sibi fortunam fingat: qui populo serviet avido, invido, ignaro, ad mutationem proclivi et, quod caput est, ingrato, ¿num aliquando beatus esse poterit? an potius, quotiens de eius naturā cogitabit, ¿totiens suam ipse calamitatem ac fortunam conqueretur?

Praeclare vetus poeta:

♫*Aeterno mixtam luctu mortalibus vitam
olim constituit divum pater atque hominum rex.*♫

[66] Itaque, quamdiu hac luce utimur, vivere quidem videmur, sed verius adsidue morimur aut saltem vitam verbo retinemus, re ipsā amisimus. Equidem non video

These downfalls keep happening, I know, and they're heartbreaking. Even more heartbreaking, though, is the man who aspires to leadership while being entirely dependent on the votes of the people. His situation is uniquely tragic. It's rife with dread, doubt, striving, with anxiety. For him, we can be sure, not an hour passes without worry. I mean, if a slave is cursed with trying to determine his fate based on the character, whim, and temperament of his master, can the man who serves a greedy, jealous, ignorant, fickle, and above all *ungrateful* people ever be happy? If he reflects on the *nature* of the masses, can he really lament his misfortune and misery?

The bard of old was right:

♫*Once, long ago, the father of gods and king of all humans*
*ordered that mortals' life be blended with heartaches unending.*[16]♫

[66] The upshot is, as long as we're enjoying the light of this world, we *think* we're alive. Really, though, we're continually dying. We're left holding the name of life, while in reality we've lost it. I myself really

quid in hominis vitā valde optandum aut felix esse possit.

Multos potius, ne in maiora quàm quae humana consuetudo cotidie fert mala inciderent, mortem sibi deditā operā conscivisse scio. (Quod tamen non idcirco dictum velim, quia probandum putem, sed ut ex eo appareat, humana vita quàm multis undique prematur difficultatibus.)

[67] Cleomenes Lacedaemoniorum rex eiusque filius morte ultro appetitā, praeterea Theagenes Numantinus, qui, ne in hostium manūs veniret, primum suis, deinde sibi ipsi mortem attulit; quanto opere vita fugienda sit, satis videntur aperte declarasse. Ac nisi turpe videatur homines a mulierculis—multo certe imbecillioribus—fortitudinis exempla petere, repetamus ex historiis Hasdrubalis uxorem illam, quae Karthagine in hostium potestatem redacta se ipsam cum tribus filiis in conflagrantis patriae incendium immisit.

[68] Sed praeter haec, quae iam testata sunt et illustria, fateamur sane ingenue tantam esse humanae naturae miseriam ut neque genus ipsum hominum nec e toto genere singuli miseriarum expertes esse possint. Quod eo magis mirandum est, quòd non iis solum malis, quibus hominis natura adsidue adfligitur, mala nostra praescripta sunt, sed ipsi nos, quantum in nobis est, miseriores cotidie reddere conamur.

don't see what could be desirable or happy in human life.

## ON SUICIDE, MUTUAL DESTRUCTION, AND HOPE

On the contrary, I know many have committed suicide to avoid bigger problems than we face in normal everyday life. (I say that *not* because I think suicide is a good idea, but to illustrate the endless pressures squeezing human life.[17])

[67] King Cleomenes [*III*] of Sparta and his son took their own lives. So did Theagenes of Numantia; he killed his loved ones, and then himself, to avoid falling into enemy hands. I'd say they declared pretty unambiguously how critical it is to get away from life. And if men can decently cite examples of fortitude in females (obviously much weaker), let's add from history the case of Hasdrubal's wife. Seeing Carthage conquered and occupied by its enemy, she flung herself and her three children into the flames of her burning country.

[68] But let's leave these famous examples aside. Let's just admit that human nature is so steeped in misery that neither the race as a whole nor individual members can be free of it. Moreover, our problems aren't even limited to those that constantly plague human nature. What's so incredible is that we do everything in our power to try to make ourselves *more* miserable every day.

Nullum enim aliud in toto terrarum orbe genus ani-
mantium reperias praeter unum hominem, quod in proprium genus atque in se ipsum saevitiam exerceat suam,
meritòque Dicaearchus in eo libro, quem "De Hominis
Interitu" luculentum et eruditum conscripsit, nihil <se>
habere dubitationis putavit quin multo plures exstincti
sint homines ipsā hominum saevitiā et acerbitate quàm
omni reliquo genere calamitatis. Tanta est enim in per-
multis avaritia, tantum ambitionis, imperii, divitiarum
studium ut explendae cupiditatis gratiā nihil sibi non lic-
ere putent. Atque hoc malum non iam angustis finibus
compressum videmus, sed superioribus saeculis erupisse
vehementer et manasse latius. Non enim certum aliquem
hominum numerum, sed regna ipsa et totas persaepe funditus sustulit civitates.

[69] At, si ad singulos homines, quae proxima ratio est,
mentem cogitationemque converteris, ne in iis quidem
quidquam reperies quod valde appetere aut approbare
possis. Finge enim animo, quidquid homini felix aut beatum ex opinione vulgari possit in vitā contingere: conge-
rantur divitiae, bona valetudo, honores, potentia, etiam
voluptates accedant: quum haec omnia in hominem
contuleris, nihil tamen tribueris stabile aut firmum, nihil
quod non repentinam et adsiduam pati mutationem
possit. Caduca enim et incerta sunt omnia, non in humanis consiliis aut viribus posita, sed in fortunae temeri-
tate ac temporum vicissitudine constituta.

You see, in all the world one cannot find a single species—apart from man alone—that engages in cruelty towards its own kind, even itself. Dicaearchus was right to be adamant, in his wonderfully informative book *On the Ruin of Man*, that many more human lives have been lost to human cruelty and savagery than to any other kind of disaster. You see, in most men the greed, the *drive* for ambition, power, and wealth is so great that they consider nothing off-limits in satisfying their lust. What's more, we've seen this scourge is no longer locally contained. In recent centuries it's erupted violently, the flow spread far and wide, and obliterated not just thousands of people, but, often enough, entire kingdoms and societies.

[69] But if you focus in on individuals, which are our primary concern, even there you won't find anything genuinely attractive or admirable. I mean, imagine every factor in life that's commonly regarded as a blessing or advantage: wealth, health, status, power, even pleasures. Give a man all this, and you *still* won't be giving him anything stable or solid, not a thing that isn't always susceptible to sudden change. Everything is fleeting and uncertain. The world heeds *not* the plans or strength of man, but the fickleness of Fortune and changing of the seasons.

[70] ¿Quid autem homini turpius quàm e temporis ac fortunae mutatione pendēre et secundo illius flatu sublevari, reflatu deprimi et adfligi? ¿aut laetis rerum eventis gloriari, adversis lugere nec lacrimis temperare posse? ¿Quid iam intersit inter hominem mutamque pecudem, si nos perinde atque illa quibus rationem natura denegavit, extrinsecus toti pendeamus, in nobis ipsis nihil fortitudinis, nihil firmitatis, nihil habeamus constantiae?

Quamvis enim homini non mater, sed verius noverca natura corpus fragile infirmumque tradiderit, animum autem et in molestiis anxium et in timore humilem et ad labores mollem, plurimos tamen insevit divinos ingenii iudiciique igniculos, quorum auxilio et cum dolore luctari et timori obsistere, labores verò omnes nullo negotio vincere ac perferre possemus. Itaque, tributum divinitus mentis ignem et prudentiae non exstinguere, sed sopitum fovere atque augere debemus.

[71] Mors autem progressis in vitā longius si immineat, nihil est cur magno opere commoveamur, quae praesertim aut meliorem quàm quo viventes fruimur, aut certe non deteriorem vitae statum sit adlatura. ¿Quis enim negabit,

[70] Picture the utter disgrace of man, dependent on the vicissitudes of time and Fortune: uplifted by tailwinds, battered and defeated by headwinds, triumphant in success, whining and weepy at failure. In what way would man differ from the brute beasts from whom Nature withheld reason if, like them, we depended entirely on externals? If we had within us no fortitude, no grit, no stamina?

You see, I know that man inherited from Mother Nature (or *Step*mother, really) a weak, brittle body, and a heart prone to stress, to sink in fear, and loathe to struggle. Yet she also seeded us with innumerable divine flashes of creativity and critical thinking. She wanted to help us grapple with pain, face down fear, and to endure and overcome every ordeal effortlessly. It's incumbent on us, therefore, *not* to extinguish the fire of Divine Intelligence and discipline granted to us, but rather, when dormant, to rekindle and fan the flames.

## TIMELY DEATH IS GOOD

[71] There's no need to fret if death comes looming when you've lived a good long time, because death will either improve our condition or at least not make it worse. Who can disagree that—?:

- si animus omnino intereat, exstincto sensu nihil esse mali, proptereaque nullam iustam doloris causam exsistere?
- at, si vigeat corpore solutus ac liber, ¿quid iam illā vitā beatius, quid divinius? ex quo, maxima et verissima laetitiae ac voluptatis exoritur occasio.

[72] Itaque, nihil iam restat quominus optimam esse mortem vere adfirmare possimus; tantumque abesse ut quum adest dolenda sit, ut numquam fugienda, saepe etiam optanda videatur; atque eo magis quo diutius in vitā homo permanserit. Nam, quum iis bonis quae adferre vita potest, satiari coeperit, tum ab humanis molestiis secedens, in beatissimam vitam commigrabit.

Non enim is ego sum, qui animum simul cum homine interire putem tantumque mentis lumen e divinā naturā delibatum posse exstingui, sed potius—certo tempore emenso—ad immortalitatem redire.

[73] ¿Quid autem hominem magis deceat quàm tam multis tamque firmis rationibus nixum virilem animum retinere, femineam mollitiem exuere? Qui verò mortuos

- If the soul dies completely, then once consciousness is extinguished, nothing bad exists, and hence there's no legitimate occasion for suffering.
- If the soul *does* survive and thrive out of its bodily prison, what could be more blessed or heavenly than the dawning of a life that brings the *truest* occasion for happiness and joy?

[72] Accordingly, nothing prevents us any longer from affirming that death really *is* the greatest good; that far from grieving when it comes, we must never run, and sometimes even opt for it; and all the more so, the longer you live. By then, you'll have had enough of all the good that life can bring, and by freeing yourself of human problems, you'll move on to a life of perfect bliss.

You see, I am not one to think the soul dies with the person and that this great light of intelligence, sampled from God's nature, *can* be extinguished. *I* believe that after a certain time, it returns to immortality.

## Pain and Adversity Breed Fortitude

### ON PROPER GRIEVING

[73] When you're equipped with all these solid arguments, nothing's more impressive than maintaining masculine courage and eliminating female

nimis lugent nec humanam condicionem magno ela-
toque animo despicere possunt, in eos illud probri ple-
num vere dicetur:

♪*Vos etenim iuvenes animum geritis muliebrem,*
*illaque virgo viri.*♪

Multae enim repertae feminae sunt, quae in domestico
luctu singularem animi praesentiam ac magnitudinem
praestiterunt.

Sed virilis fortitudo, ut libidini, sic dolori non aliter
quàm servo domina imperare debet, eamque coercere ac
frangere tamquam vitiosam et imbecillam animi partem.
Quam si emergere patiatur seque paulo altius efferre, non
modo rationi praecurret, sed etiam victrix in animo ex-
sultabit. Quo nihil homini turpius aut perniciosius, ne ex-
cogitari quidem possit.

[74] Gorgias orator, iam aetate confectus ac morti
proximus, rogatus num libenter moreretur:

"Maxime verò (*inquit*), nam tamquam ex putri
miserāque domo laetus egredior."

emotionality. Those who grieve their dead in excess lack the bold and lofty perspective needed to despise the human condition. They'll rightfully hear the famous taunt applied to themselves:

> ♫ You *"tough" guys are displaying the mindset*
>   *and heart of a woman.*
> She *is as tough as a man!*♫

Because, of course, we *have* seen many examples of women that have shown a singular presence of mind and greatness of soul amid their private grief.

But as with lust, *masculine* mental toughness ought to *rule* over pain, precisely as master does slave. It should constrain and crush pain, like a flawed and weak part of the soul, which, if allowed an outlet, will not only forestall reason, but even run rampant in the soul in triumph. I can't even imagine anything more disgraceful or pernicious for a man.

[74] When the public intellectual Gorgias was wracked with age and at death's door, he was asked whether he was okay with dying. He replied,

> "Thrilled!—it's like I'm moving out of a rotten, crummy house."[18]

¡O virum egregium, dignumque cuius vigeat in omnium ore ac mente sententia! ¿Quid enim potuit praeclarius dicere, quum mala quae viventem pati necesse est cogitaret, miseriarum finem quas moriens relinquebat, adesse laetaretur? Sic par est loqui hominem qui non libidine vexetur, non voluptatis illecebris irretiatur, nulli denique pareat cupiditati: quae summa est ratio et sapientia, humanae necessitati imperare, non dolori cedere, non desiderio angi, nihil denique humanum extimescere.

[75] ¿Angamur liberorum aut adfinium interitu? ¿Quid ita? ¿ut stultos imitemur, qui quae mutari non possunt quaeque vel nolentes opprimunt, perferre nequeunt? ¿saniores, quorum tam multa exstant ad aeternitatem illustria sive exempla sive testimonia, negligamus? ¿Quid est aliud caecorum more ambulare et, quum in celebritate versari ac solis lumine uti possis, solitudinem tamen ac tenebras quaerere? Iam enim ad eos, quos aemulari satius est quosque nobis imitandos proposuit antiquitas, nostra delabatur oratio.

[76] Mortem igitur in malis nullo modo esse ponendam, sed in praecipuis bonis numerandam dubitaturum puto neminem:

Epic man! He deserves to have that quip echo through the ages. I mean, what nobler response could he have given? He weighed the downsides that living entailed and was happy that dying meant a blissful end to all the misery. *That* is the proper response for a man who's no prisoner of his appetites, isn't hooked on pleasure, who ignores every craving; and *that*, in turn, is the sum and substance of reason and wisdom: taking charge of human nature, not giving in to pain, not growing anguished with longing, and, in sum, dreading no part of the human condition.

[75] *Should* we despair at the death of children or relatives? Why? To act like fools—unable to endure what we cannot change, and getting overwhelmed despite ourselves? Just *ignore* all those magnificent precedents and testimonies we have from wiser heads that echo through the ages!? How's that different from walking with your eyes closed? Or from preferring, when you could be out enjoying life with friends, to sit alone in the dark? I ask because antiquity has come up with *positive* role models for us to follow, and it's with them that I'll now deal in my essay.

[76] By no means, therefore, should we classify death as bad. Rather, it must be considered one of our greatest goods, and I don't think we can doubt it, because:

- If death delivers us from miseries, leads to a better life, isn't itself miserable, and plays no role in misery, then why call it bad?
- If, on the contrary, death empowers us to obtain everlasting blessings and gain eternal life (a life we assumed was mortal), then what could be happier?

## A MODEL RESPONSE

Hence we hear that, far from becoming grief-stricken or in any way upset at the death of loved ones, the wisest among us often rejoiced. [77] Tradition has it that news of his son's death reached Anaxagoras while he was lecturing among friends on the nature of the universe, and his only response was,

"I knew he was mortal when I begot him."

A brilliant remark, truly worthy of such a great man! I really don't see what one could say to express greater wisdom or strength of mind. Should he have said:—?

- "He died young!" But that would have been the sign of a broken heart, not determination in the face of adversity.

- ¿An angi sese non suā, sed filii causā? ¿Num igitur ignorare se fateretur quantis e malis elapsus esset filius?
- ¿An se quidem dolere, sed tamen humanum casum agnoscere? ¿Ubi ergo hominis gravitas, iudicium, sapientia, aut ¿quid ab imperitorum turbā distabit? e quibus tamen saepe multi nec iis rebus anguntur quae necessariò eveniunt, nec quominus eveniant, quum communes omnibus sint, laborandum ullo pacto censent.

[78] Ille verò sapiens et vere philosophus, quem neque improvisus nuntius perculit nec a disputatione abduxit, sed potius vocem expressit summae indicem fortitudinis ac sapientiae.

Vellem et hoc ipsum de pluribus ex nostris dicere liceret: quos si qua interdum fortunae oppressit iniuria, nihil aliud iudices quàm prostratos illos ac penitus abiectos esse. ¡Quasi verò aliquid acciderit, quod vel ante ipsos nemini aut quod ipsis, si minus hoc tempore, saltem paucis post annis non eventurum fuerit! Ac, quum maxime animo vigere deberent, tum praecipue non solum praeteritae patriaeque virtutis, sed etiam humanae legis ac paene obliviscuntur sui. Tantum in eorum animis mollities potest ac servitus quaedam doloris atque tristitiae.

- "I grieve not for myself, but for my son." But wouldn't that mean admitting he didn't *know* what horrors his son had escaped?
- "It does hurt, but I recognize that tragedy is part of life." In that case, what would become of his sobriety, his discernment, his wisdom? How would he be any different from the uneducated masses? (Many of whom, incidentally, are often untroubled by the inevitable and see no point in trying to prevent something we all have to go through.)

[78] No, he behaved like a wise and true *philosopher*. Far from the sudden news fazing or distracting him from his lecture, he spoke words that revealed consummate fortitude and wisdom.

I wish I could say the same for most of us! When many people are involved in some minor accident, you'd think they're crushed, devastated — as if what's happened were totally unprecedented or weren't bound to happen to them sooner or later! Just when they *should* be at their toughest, they go so far as to forget, not only the resilience that they and their forefathers showed in the past, but even the laws of human nature and almost their very selves. Such is what mental softness, and bondage to grief, have wrought.

[79] ¿An ego illum iudicare liberum possim, cui dolor imperat? quem repentinus casus perturbat, impellit, evertit, qui nihil prae doloris magnitudine cogitare, nihil meditari queat? qui nihil in se ipso, in temporibus atque in fortunā, quae stabilitatis nihil habet, sua ponat omnia? Ego verò istam non modo servitutem, sed paene captivitatem et quidem miserrimam censuerim.

¿Quid enim interest inter eum qui vinctus ab hostibus et carceribus conclusus obsideatur, et eum qui dolore captus suo prorsus careat arbitrio?

- At ille quidem, etsi corpore serviat, animo tamen liber est nec dubitat aliquando fore ut libertatem adsequatur.
- Qui verò dolori paret, nec valet corpore et animo quàm maxime laborat. Non enim amicis frui, non rei publicae prodesse, non privatas res curare, non publicis consulere potest. Ita in otio et quidem molestissimo nec cuiquam paret et tamen sibi non imperat.

Qui quum adsiduis et maximis prematur angustiis, alterum esse necesse est, ut, quamdiu in dolore versatur, semper miser sit; alterum fieri nullo modo potest ut, nisi

## AUTONOMY IN GRIEF

[79] Could I legitimately say you "have autonomy" if you're in thrall to grief? If you get troubled, worked up, devastated by a sudden blow? If, in the depths of despair, you cannot think or concentrate on anything? If you believe you're completely powerless and attribute everything to structural causes and the randomness of luck? I for one wouldn't call that just slavery, but virtually imprisonment, and of the worst possible kind.

I mean, what's the difference between getting arrested and locked up and guarded by enemies in jail, and getting caught up in grief and having no will of your own? Well,

- In the first scenario, even if your body's enslaved, at least your heart is still free, and you don't doubt that freedom is coming.
- As a slave of *grief*, though, you're physically impaired *and* suffering unimaginable heartache. You can't enjoy friends, serve your country, manage your private life, advise the public. You have freedom, but the most oppressive kind: you answer to no one, yet don't govern yourself.

Crushed by extreme and unrelenting anxiety, you'll be miserable for however long your grief lasts. You'll *have* to be, since the alternative—regaining

dolere desinat, a miseriis eximatur.

[80] ¡Quanto sapientius Xenophon! Qui, quum sacra sollemnia perageret maioremque natu filium in proelio apud Mantineam cecidisse audiret, coronam tantum e capite deposuit, sed in sacris peragendis constanter perstitit. Ubi verò cognovit fortiter pugnantem occidisse, coronam rursus capiti imposuit deosque ipsos, quibus litabatur, testatus est maiorem se ex filii virtute voluptatem quàm ex obitu molestiam cepisse.

Huic ego non dubitarim quin omnia, quaecumque accidere possent in vitā, nullam essent perturbationem adlatura. Qui enim usque eo in deorum cultu constans et firmus esset ut neque filii morte nuntiatā ab iis avocari posset, ¿cur eum credam filii morte lugendā a deorum voluntate dissensurum fuisse? aut qui virtutem filii vitae anteferret, ¿non iure credi possit illum et virtutis studio incensum et patriae caritate impulsum omnes molestias omnesque calamitates libentissime fuisse subiturum?

[81] Sed quo rariores qui hoc modo animati sint, hoc praeclariores viri. Nihil enim ad laudem illustrius quàm in aeternam gloriam aut in patriae utilitatem intuentem aut saltem fortiter dolores perferentem et cum fortunā

independence without ending the grieving process—is utterly impossible.

[80] Xenophon was so much wiser! While performing a sacrifice, he received word that his older son
had fallen in battle at Mantinea. He removed the
garland from his head, but he manfully continued
performing the sacrifice. When he then heard he'd
fallen fighting *bravely*, though, Xenophon put the
garland back on, and called the gods he was pray-
ing to as witness that his son's *death* brought him
less pain than his *heroism* did joy.

I'd readily believe that *nothing* that can happen
in life would have troubled that man. I mean, a man
*so* resolute and unwavering in his worship of the
gods that not even news of his son's death could distract him—how could I think he'd argue with the
will of the gods by mourning his son's death? Can't
we conclude that if a man preferred his son's heroism to his life, that when fired with valor and im-
pelled by patriotism, he'd have eagerly endured any
hardship, any tragedy?

[81] And the rarer such-minded heroes are, the
more magnificent they are. You see, when you're
bent on immortal glory, patriotic duty, or simply
coping with pain and struggling with misfortune

luctantem negligere humana. Quae qui nimium curant, ii laudis studium, civium commoda, denique omnia quae laudabilia putantur, prorsus e mente ac cogitatione eiiciant, necesse est.

Neque enim humanis curis implicitus toto animo de patriae salute atque utilitate cogitare aut laudem sibi praeclaris actionibus comparare vel egregii quidquam suscipere ac sustinere queat. Suis autem commodis ac rationibus prospiciens et consulens cetera omittet, de se ipso dies noctesque cogitabit. Ita nec boni civis nec boni viri fungetur officio. Bonum enim virum decet de ceterorum commodis aeque laborare ac de suis, bonum verò civem sua omnia posteriora habere, patriae commoda prima et maxima ducere; a quibus neque dolore neque ullā omnino humanā avelli perturbatione debemus.

[82] Periclem narrant historiae intra quadriduum duobus filiis, eximiae indolis adolescentibus, esse orbatum. Qui usque eo fortis ac constans in luctu fuit ut nihil prorsus de pristino habitu cultuque deminuerit, sed eundem quem antea in contionibus habendis morem ritumque servarit nec umquam coronam e capite deposuerit. De quo traditum est, nihil eum putavisse indignius futurum quàm si aliquod fracti animi signum maeroris causā muliebri more edidisset.

¡Fortem sane hominem, et magnā laude aeternāque memoriā dignissimum! Quem neque naturae vis ad

manfully, *nothing* is more ennobling than a disregard for human needs. People who worry too much about them have no choice; they must suppress all thought of competitiveness, duty, or *anything* high-minded.

You see, if you're wholeheartedly obsessed with human concerns, you *cannot* think of saving or helping your country, winning praise for amazing achievements, or taking on and executing a major project. You'll ignore everything else if you're looking out for your *own* advantages, your *own* wallet. You'll be thinking night and day of yourself. You'll be neither patriot nor a real man, since a real man serves the interests of others as much as his own, while a patriot puts his own interests second and prioritizes those of his country—and from those interests, no grief or human troubles should ever distract us.

[82] Pericles, says history, lost two sons—extraordinary young men—in four days. He was so strong and unwavering in his grief, though, that he didn't change a single thing in his conduct or appearance. On the contrary, he kept to his schedule of public meetings and never removed the garland from his head. We're told he thought nothing would be more compromising than to reveal, as women do, any sign of grief or anguish.

What a hero, worthy of all our praise and everlasting memory! The power of nature could not

nimium saepe amorem trahens potuerit de statu dimovere et ad dolorem abducere nec liberorum desiderium, quos tamen summe dilexisse dicitur, ullā ratione perturbarit.

[83] Nec mirum. Vera enim fortitudo inanes sollicitudines eiicit ac depellit, opprimit cupiditates, imperat timori, nihil autem appetit forti viro indignum nec ab ullā re vel metu vel inconstantiā repellitur. Et quamvis excelsam elatamque naturam ratio ipsa doctrinae praeceptis imbuta confirmet—quod Pericli doctissimo homini maximoque ingenio praedito sine ullā dubitatione contigisse prorsus mihi persuadeo—ipsae tamen fortitudinis radices in animo praecipue insident. Qui quum humana despicit nec ad humilia quasi humi depressus ullo pacto adhaerescit, facile fit ut uberiores et maturiores fructūs ferat, quum ad eum, veluti ad agrum optimum cultura, ratio etiam accesserit conformatioque doctrinae.

Non enim sensu omni doloris caruisse summos viros credendum est. ¿Qualis enim nihil sentientis animi sensūsque prorsus carentis esse fortitudo potuisset? Sed dolorem sentientes ad eum opprimendum ac vincendum summam animi contentionem adhibebant tantumque nitebantur ut e pugnā discederent superiores.

destabilize *him*, not make *him* grief-stricken, though it often makes us too attached. And the longing for his children—though we're told he loved them deeply—also failed to shake him in any way.

[83] And that's not surprising, since true fortitude repels and banishes pointless anxieties. It quashes desires, controls dread, wants nothing unworthy of a real man, is deterred from nothing by fear or wavering.[19] And although clear thinking, combined with education, can *strengthen* a natural predisposition to greatness—which was the case, I'm convinced beyond all doubt, with Pericles, a man endowed with extraordinary learning *and* genius—nevertheless, fortitude itself is first and foremost rooted in the *heart*. When your heart despises human concerns and refuses to be abased or dragged down, it easily comes to bear healthier and more abundant fruits. It does so because you've applied clear thought and education to it, the same way cultivation improves an excellent piece of land.

We must not imagine that our heroes *felt* no grief at all; I mean, what sort of fortitude could reside in a heart that feels nothing or lacks all sensation? Rather, it was *while feeling grief* that they made a heroic mental effort to conquer and crush it, and they struggled so valiantly that they walked away the victors.

[84] You see, it's true what they say, that *no greater bane can befall the heart than a moment's letting up.*

- When the mind remains taut and braced for impact, it bears every burden, swats down even speeding bullets.
- When it's weakened and unmanned by letting up, by contrast, it becomes so distraught and depressed that it cannot regain its balance.

You'd never be able to face and endure a bout of grief manfully if you hadn't steeled yourself for impact in advance. You'd never be able to learn mental toughness if you hadn't fought back pain many times in the past. [85] Those struggles breed habituation, which toughens the heart and arms us against every blow of Nature or Fortune.

Could Harpagus the Mede have furnished the striking example of fortitude recorded by Herodotus [*Histories 1.119–129*] if he hadn't repeatedly practiced endurance and mental toughness in advance? And didn't it pay off in spades, and to his eternal credit? His ability to play the long game was *so* superior that he endured the bitterest outrage without any visible sign of grief, and he succeeded in repaying the king's sadism with interest.

Nam, quum eius filium rex Astyages interfectum ad epulandum apponi iussisset caputque ei post cenam adlatum ostendisset, rogans cuius ferae viscera in mensā comedisset, ille verò nihil perterritus nec animo ullam in partem deiecto,

"Agnosco (*inquit*) quid sit actum ac, quidquid regi placuit, mihi quoque placere pronuntio."

Hoc autem immanissimum genus iniuriae tam diu dissimulavit, quoad Cyrum ex Persiā in Mediam evocare potuit; quo adveniente—quum exercitūs imperator contra eum a rege missus esset—et regnum et regem illi tradidit. Itaque, Astyages in Cyri potestatem, impietatis suae poenas daturus, redactus est.

[86] ¡O factum omnium gentium ac saeculorum memoriā dignissimum! ex quo non modo qui dolori cedunt ad patientiam ac fortitudinem excitentur, sed etiam reges quique hominibus imperant, ne quid impium aut indecens audeant, erudiantur. Nam adversùs iniustitiam atque impietatem tantum est odium, tanta invidia ut ne ipsum quidem caelum aut sidera, etiam si homines velint, huius modi scelera pati ac dissimulare possint. Ac, si sera deorum vindicta sit, noluerunt tamen impios ipso in facinore adeo exsultare ut non angore conscientiae fraudisque cruciatu tamquam domesticis Furiis adsidue

You see, the king, Astyages, had ordered Harpagus' son killed and served for dinner. After the meal, the king had the head brought in and shown to Harpagus, and asked, "What kind of meat do you think you were eating?" Harpagus didn't panic, didn't flinch. He simply said,

"I see what's been done, and let it be known that
all that pleases the king, pleases me as well."

He then hid his horror at this outrage until such time as he could call Cyrus [*the Great*] of Persia in to Media. And when Cyrus drew near—since Harpagus had been dispatched to lead the army against him—he handed Cyrus both kingdom and king. So it is that Astyages was made prisoner to Cyrus to pay for his sin.

[86] Now *there*'s a lesson for all mankind, for the ages! Let it inspire those wallowing in grief to get tough and endure. Let it also be a warning to kings and authorities not to abuse their power wantonly— because outrageous abuses are so hated, *so* resented, that even if humans remained silent in the face of such crimes, the very sky and stars above could not. The gods may delay vengeance, true, but they refused to let abusers celebrate getting away with their crimes; abusers feel pangs of guilt and remorse, like demons inside, constantly harassing

vexentur. [87] Tantumque potest impietatis odium ut tyrannum exstinctum ac saevissime excruciatum nemo misereatur, nemo doleat. Nam adversùs hoc hominum genus nec in ullo praeterea omnem prorsus vim omnesque stimulos amittit dolor.

Qui si ratione comprimendus est, quod supra diximus, multo etiam magis consuetudine vincetur, cuius tantae sunt vires ut non modo perturbationes animi sedare, sed etiam naturae vim adferre, eamque saepissime immutare ac penitus aliam possit efficere. Cuius auxilio non modo doloris aculei, sed etiam fortunae fulmina depelli ac contemni facile poterunt.

Meditemur igitur et omnino statuamus nihil prorsus humanum esse dolendum,

- non mortem, quam iam optimam esse cognovimus,
- non egestatem, quae saepissime maximi boni causā a dis immortalibus tribuatur,
- non exsilium, quum orbis terrarum omnibus pateat,
- non cetera generis eiusdem quae vulgi opinione gravissimis in malis numerantur.

Nullum enim tam grave malum apparebit quin ex eo bonum aliquod multo maius multoque optabilius magno

them. [87] In fact, fury at abuse is so overwhelming that no one pities or grieves the horrific torture or killing of a tyrant. Against such people—and no other—grief simply loses all its power, and stops cold.

If clear thinking is the way to *stifle* grief, as I've said [*section 83*], then *habituation* will actually help *overcome* it. The force of habit is such that it not only calms emotions, it can even hack Nature, and often even change her entirely. Habit will help us brush off not only acute pain but even freak accidents, and laugh at them.

## SUMMARY, RECAPITULATION, AND FURTHER EXAMPLES

Let's therefore reflect and agree, once and for all, that absolutely no human tragedy should afflict us:

- Not death, which we now know is the greatest good [*sections 58, 72, 76*].
- Not poverty, which the immortal gods often bestow as a great blessing.
- Not exile, since all the world is our homeland.
- Not anything else of the sort the masses call their worst nightmares.

You see, nothing will happen so dire that—thanks to the gods' great kindness—it doesn't ultimately

deorum beneficio aliquando colligatur. Pleni sunt libri philosophorum, refertae argumentis ac rationibus paginae fere omnes, tanta autem exemplorum copia ut nihil possit esse cumulatius. [88] Quae quum ita sint, ¿qua iam re terreamur aut cui dolori cedamus?

Dion certe, qui e Platonis scholā defluxit, quum eius filius in atrium e tecto delapsus interisset, non modo non doluit, sed etiam in eo quod tum forte agebat, constanter perstitit. Quo facto iudicavit et vir sapiens et Platonis discipulus quid ceteros qui sapientes haberi volunt, facere oporteat.

[89] At Praexaspes [*Riccoboni* : Traheaspes *printed editions*] multo fortius, siquidem filii morientis, quum ferro traiiceretur, sine ullo prorsus dolore spectator fuit. Cambyses enim iratus et ebrius quum eius filium sagittis peteret iamque pectus reclusum appareret, patrem iussit inspicere num cor percussum esset. Cui quum pater respondisset iam cordi sagittam esse infixam, tum Cambyses, "¿Numquid certam," inquit, "habeo manum?" At pater nullo doloris signo dato nec usquam conversā aut commotā facie,

"Ne Apollinem quidem (*inquit*) certiores sagittas emissurum crediderim."

net you some much greater and more desirable good. The books of philosophers are packed, practically every page *crammed*, with proofs and reasons, while illustrative examples are piled sky-high. [88] Given that reality, what's there to fear? Why wallow in grief ever again?

For example, Dion [*tyrant of Syracuse, 408–354 BCE*] was a product of Plato's Academy. When his son fell from the roof into the atrium and died, not only did he *not* grieve, he even steadfastly continued the proceedings he had started. In so doing, that wise disciple of Plato's set the example of wisdom for all others.

[89] That said, Prexaspes showed far *greater* fortitude. *He* was made to watch his son die—shot in the chest—and remained emotionless; Cambyses [*II, King of Persia*] was drunk and had been angrily taking shots at his son. Cambyses then had the boy's chest slit open and told the father to check and see if he'd reached the heart. "Yes," the father answered. "The arrow is sticking out of his heart." "Do I, or do I not, have a sure hand?" Cambyses asked. Showing no sign of grief or distress and never dropping his gaze, the father replied,

> "Even *Apollo* couldn't have shot straighter,
> I don't think."

¿Quid hunc patrem putemus facturum fuisse, si filius in pugnā fortiter dimicans occubuisset, qui nullius culpae conscium filium crudelissime trucidari non doluerit? ¿Num credamus filii mortem honestam ac pro patriā susceptam tali patri futuram fuisse iucundissimam? Nec tamen dubito permultos fore, qui impium illum ac paene viscerum suorum carnificem vocent. Sed faciant sane ut lubet, dum hoc mihi concedant, exemplum hoc fortitudinis ac devicti doloris esse praeclarissimum.

[90] Quod si ita est ut infirmos animos spectata ceterorum virtus erigat et confirmet, ¿quem censeamus iam dolori concessurum, quum tam multos audiat, qui se ipsos in dolore superarint?

Quocirca, tam multa veterum exempla colligere vereor ne supervacaneum aut fortasse putidum videatur. Quod si ceteris tantum et non nobismet ipsis scriberemus, fortasse breves [*Le Clerc* : breviores *printed editions*] in scribendo, in exemplis autem recensendis etiam breviores [*Le Clerc* : priores *printed editions*] essemus.

Sed fit nescioquomodo ut ex aliorum casibus ad mala nostra sananda medicinam colligamus. Nobis quidem ita videtur, et, quum nostro vulneri medeamur, mirari non debebunt, qui haec in manūs sument, si quid fortasse paulo expressum uberius invenerint. [91] Illud certe propositum habemus, ut omnibus nobiscum prodesse

This father didn't grieve the cold-blooded murder of a son who'd done nothing wrong. How should we imagine him reacting if his son had fallen fighting bravely in battle? Wouldn't such a dad be *thrilled* with his son's honorable, patriotic death? There are many, I know, who'd call him obscene, practically the executioner of his own flesh and blood. Well, let them, as long as they grant me he's a perfect illustration of fortitude overcoming grief.

## ON THE COMFORT OF PRECEDENT

[90] If faint hearts really *are* inspired and reassured by examples of others' courage, then who will still wallow in grief upon learning that so many have gotten over grief on their own?

I do worry that collecting all these old anecdotes [*cf. section 4*] will seem pointless, even annoying. And if I were writing only for others, and not myself, I probably *would* provide only a few arguments, and even fewer examples.

But it somehow does happen that in others' tragedies, I'm finding remedies for my problems—or so it seems to me, at least, and since it's *my* wound I'm healing, those who pick this book up shouldn't be surprised if anything strikes them as a little overwrought. [91] That was my plan. I want to help myself and everyone else simultaneously. To the

omniumque dolori, quàm accuratissime fieri possit, consolationem adferre possimus.

Quamobrem, his enumerandis nostram valde imminui atque adlevari molestiam experimur; ceteris idem optamus ac, si dicere liceat, etiam speramus. Nam in tantā vel argumentorum vel exemplorum copiā quibus se legentes paene obrui sentient, ¿ecquis se immobilem aut in dolore inexorabilem praebeat?

[*Desunt nonnulla*]

[92] Nec verò ignoro nonnulla interdum accidere, quibus ita perturbetur et opprimatur animus ut a medicinā refugiat, idque si ullo in casu contingit, certe, quum dolore adfligimur, maxime solet evenire. Quod ex eo fit, quod erepti vel amici vel adfinis vel filii cogitatio adeo nobis grata est, quod illum paene ante oculos constituere videatur ut, etiam si dolorem refricet et lacrimas eliciat, tamen eam deponere nolimus. Ac, si ad consolandum remedia suppetant, tamen nihil minus quàm consolantium verba audiamus. Falluntur sane graviter, qui ita agunt, sed hunc errorem, quo magno opere delectantur, sibi extorqueri nolunt.

extent I can, I also aim to offer *comprehensive* consolation for everyone's grief.

Hence, I'm finding that listing these examples greatly reduces and alleviates my pain. I want the same for others, and even dare hope it will. I mean, with this almost dizzying array of arguments and case studies, could *anyone* suffering from grief that's reading these pages remain unmoved—remain beyond help?

[*Gap in the text here*]

[92] . . . that said, I realize accidents do sometimes happen which leave the heart so overwhelmed and flustered that it resists treatment; and if there's ever a case where that happens, it tends to occur most when we're stricken with grief. Why? Because thinking of a lost friend or relative or child makes us *so* happy—because it feels like the person is practically standing before our eyes—that even though thinking of them rips the pain back open and makes us cry, we still don't want to stop. Worse, even if therapies are available to console us, there's still nothing we'd rather hear less than voices of consolation. Those who react this way are sorely mistaken, of course, but the mistake makes them so happy they won't give it up.

[93] Quare, suum uni cuique studium suaque omnibus delectatio relinquatur. Non enim vereor quin, si minus in ipso doloris aestu remediis utendum homines censeant, certe, quum modice dolor resederit ac se paulum quasi remittere coeperit, ad exstinguendas doloris reliquias monita praeceptaque nostra adhibeantur.

Nihil autem utilius est quàm haec eadem in voluptate ac laetitiā pertractare atque in manibus habere. Sic enim et legi atque ad verbum edisci et penitus memoriae mandari possunt ut, quum in animum penitus influxerint, tum exhauriri ac prorsus elabi non facile queant. [94] Ita, fit ut quum repente dolor invasit, tum iis utamur; quae—nisi ante percepta et cognita sint—impetu ipso doloris incurrente plane depelli atque excludi solent.

Sensimus hoc in nobis ipsis, nec parum nobis obfuit hanc universam adversùs dolorem commentationem non multo ante animo ac mente percurrisse. Quamvis enim permultos philosophorum libros vel "De Luctu" vel "De Morte" satis accurate legissemus, ut Theophrasti, Xenocratis, aliorum quos commemorare nihil attinet, tamen hoc non ideo feceramus, quòd eventurum putaremus, ut iis ipsis in nostro maerore uteremur. Itaque, neque

[93] So, let's let each person keep what works for them, each their illusion. I mean, if people say not to use remedies in the very throes of grief [*in section 1*], well, once the grief has partially subsided and started letting up a bit, I'm certainly not worried about them using my strategies and rules to stamp out what grief remains.

## THE BENEFITS OF PRACTICE

Moreover, there's nothing more useful than studying and keeping these strategies near in times of joy and happiness. That way, people can read and review and memorize them, because once they internalize them, they can't easily lose or forget them. [94] That way, too, if grief attacks suddenly, we'll apply them reflexively. And that's good, because if we haven't taken them in and understood them in advance, the violent incursion of grief itself tends to totally forestall and block them out.

That was my own experience, and, without question, not internalizing this whole "anti-grief" science far in advance did hurt me. You see, I'd read a great many philosophy books titled *Grief* or *On Death*, such as those by Theophrastus, Xenocrates, and others there's no point naming, and relatively carefully. However, I didn't read them in the thought that I might one day use them for my own

lectionem quantum oportuisset accuratam nec memoriam satis intentam adhibuimus. Casu autem repentino oppressi, non prius ad libros confugere potuimus quin ante acerbitatis vi prosterneremur.

Quamquam, postea tempore ipso factum est ut dolor nec ut antea acrior, et mens ipsa paulo esset sedatior et ad medicinam accipiendam magis idonea.

[95] Sed pergamus ad reliqua, quae nec multa restant, et scitu ac cognitione dignissima; fructu autem ipso, quem praecipue quaerimus, gratiora fortasse et uberiora.

¿Quid est, ergo, quod aliquam nobis adferre dubitationem possit, cur nihil omnino nostrorum morte dolere debeamus? Credo, si quando nobis in mentem venit magnam nos ex eorum quos amisimus operā ac studio utilitatem percepturos fuisse. At hoc non ad amicos aut adfines quorum dolere videmur interitu, sed ad nosmet ipsos pertinebit. Mercennarius igitur dolor fuerit quique non ex adfinitate aut benevolentiā, sed ex unā proveniat utilitate. ¿Quid autem flagitiosius et indignius quàm eum qui sic doleat fateri oportere, quum tanto opere alicuius morte crucietur, quòd aliquā utilitate privatus sit, si nihil

sorrows, so I didn't read them as carefully or re-member them as vividly as they deserved. When tragedy blindsided me, I couldn't get to the books before finding myself floored by the shocking pain.

> And yet it's true that time *did* later make the pain less acute, and my mind a little calmer and in a better state to accept treatment.

[95] But let's keep going. There aren't many more examples and they're absolutely worth our atten-tion, while the results—which are what we're really after—may well enrich and enhance the reading.

## GRIEF IS ILLOGICAL

What could shake our conviction that the death of loved ones just isn't a cause for grief? The idea, pos-sibly, that we'd have garnered some great benefit from the support of those we've lost? But that thought would pertain to *ourselves*, not the friends or relatives whose passing we think we're grieving. In that case, grief would be up for rent. It would result not from family ties or love, but self-interest. Now, imagine the grief-stricken man who's shat-tered by someone's death because he feels he's lost out on some self-interest. Could anything be more pathetic or disgraceful than him admitting that if he *hadn't* hoped to get some advantage from the

ex eius vitā beneficii ac commodi se consecuturum spe-
ravisset, nihil sibi omnino dolendum fuisse?

[96] At videamus non Persas aut Scythas, sed e mediā civitate nostrā clarissimos et praestantissimos viros ac
cives qui non modo amicorum cum quibus coniunctis-
sime vixerant, sed etiam liberorum et quidem carissimo-
rum interitum ita fortiter et constanter tulerunt ut causae
nihil sit quin eos superioribus Graecis comparare atque
etiam anteferre debeamus. Atque hoc multo magis in illis
mirandum fuerit, quòd in eorum obitu se fortissimos et
constantissimos praebuerunt qui, non modo ipsis utilis-
simi, si vixissent, sed paene soli utiles ac iucundi esse po-
tuissent. ¿Quid enim utilius filio, ¿quid iucundius unico?

[1] [97] At filium et unicum Q. Fabius, praeterea consularem, qui iam magnas res gesserat et maiores cogita-
bat, amisit. Neque solum non doluit, quòd fortissimi
animi fuit, sed etiam mortuo laudationem in Foro dixit;
quo nihil fortius aut laudabilius ne ex omni quidem

deceased continuing to live, there'd be no point in him feeling bad at all?

## Profiles in Courage

### ANCIENT EXAMPLES OF ROMAN FORTITUDE

[96] Let's now look not to Persians or Scythians, but to glorious heroes and statesmen right here in our own country who not only lost their nearest and dearest friends, but even their precious children. They survived those losses with such stamina and fortitude that there's no reason *not* to compare, even prefer, them to the Greeks mentioned above. Indeed, on one score they're far ahead: namely, those whose deaths summoned forth such displays of stamina and fortitude not only would have been a great help to their parents if they'd lived, they were virtually their parents' *only* source of help and delight. Because what's more helpful than a child, or more delightful than an *only* child?

[*1*] [97] Quintus Fabius [*Maximus Verrucosus, Consul, third century BCE*] lost a son—his only son, and a former Consul to boot—who'd accomplished great things and was planning greater. Yet not only did he *not* grieve (which already heralds great fortitude), he even delivered his son's eulogy in the Forum. No finer example of fortitude can be

antiquitate recenseri potest. Cuius orationem ¿quis non admiretur, insignem ingenii, iudicii, ordinis praestantia? quomodo ille vel ea quae dixit sine luctu dicere aut quae scripsit sine dolore cogitare potuit? quum praesertim hoc in illā laudatione et admirari et obstipescere soleamus, quod non ut alii, de ceterorum fortitudine disputat ut suum ipse dolorem aliorum exemplo minuat, sed in filio haerens illius maxime virtutes propriasque laudes, quae vel acerbiorem efficere doloris sensum poterant, longissimo sermone persequitur.

[2] [98] Quod singularis virtutis exemplum fortasse Horatii Pulvilli laudem magnā ex parte deminuere videatur; quem tamen summum virum silentio praeterire nefas ducimus, quum in eo ipso—quòd filii mortem aequissimo ac fortissimo animo tulit—etiam Iovi optimo maximo, cuius aedem dedicabat, gratissimum fecisse videatur. Nam pontifex inter sollemnium verborum nuncupationem postem tenens ut filium mortuum audivit, neque manum a poste removit, ne sacra dirimeret, nec vultum a populo avertit, ne suum potius dolorem quàm populi utilitatem ac salutem cogitare videretur.

[3] [99] Iam ¿quid L. Paullo insignius, quid illustrius? qui filios paucissimis diebus duos ita perdidit ut nullum

found in all of history! And the *speech*! Who doesn't
admire its inspiration, its taste, its clarity? How did
he deliver it without crying, or write it without col-
lapsing? Because the most awe-inspiring thing
about it is the unusual tack he took. Instead of cit-
ing famous examples of fortitude to help himself
cope with his grief, he lingers on his son. He ex-
pounds the son's talents and achievements at great
length—and that can only have exacerbated his
anguish.

[2] [98] That unprecedented example of mettle
might seem to eclipse the eulogy given by [*Marcus*]
Horatius Pulvillus [*Consul, sixth century BCE*].
Still, it seems wrong to pass over that towering man
in silence. He too endured the death of a son, and
with such fortitude and composure that he evidently impressed Jupiter Optimus Maximus himself. Pulvillus was Pontiff, you see, and dedicating
His temple at the time. He was uttering the sacred
words and touching the doorpost when he got word
his son had died. Not only did Pulvillus *not* with-
draw his hand (so as not to invalidate the ritual); he
didn't even avert his gaze from the people, for fear
of seeming to care more for his own grief than the
general welfare of the people.

[3] [99] What case is more famous or celebrated
than Lucius [*Aemilius*] Paullus [*Consul, second
century BCE*]? He lost two sons just days apart,

paene doloris [paullo] acrioris [*Riccoboni* : acrius *printed editions*] indicium ediderit, ac potius in eā contione quam de rebus a se gestis ad populum habuit, laetatus est, quid-quid populo Romano immineret adversi, totum id in se ipsum a dis immortalibus esse conversum.

[*4*] [100] Cum Sulpicio verò Gallo ¿quis neget actum esse praeclarissime? cuius innocentiam, sapien-tiam, militarem virtutem, etiam insignis in obitu filii fortitudo illustraverit. Quem ut numquam lubens taci-tum dimiserim,

[*5*] sic ad Catonem properans exsultare videtur animus et quasi in portum ex horridā tempestate delatus in sapi-entissimi viri nomine atque exemplo conquiescere. Neque enim maiori mihi admirationi esse solent clarissimi homi-nis res gestae ac virtus non solum in luce patriae, sed etiam in congressu hostium cognita, quàm fuit illa in filii morte praetoris designati in oculis omnium civium forti-tudo declarata.

[101] Atque horum egregia in domesticis miseriis atque aerumnis facinora qui fortiter in civitate nostrā imitati sint, casūsque fortunae gravissimos patientissime tuler-int, non difficile fuerit oratione complecti.

[*6*] Nam et Q. Marcius Rex, quum unicum summae pietatis summaeque virtutis filium amisisset, dolorem

with almost no sign of grief. Rather, in the speech he gave before the people reporting on his accomplishments, he *thanked* the immortal gods for bringing down upon himself whatever adversity was threatening the Roman people!

[4] [100] Undeniably, [*Gaius*] Sulpicius Gallus [*Consul, second century BCE*] lived a truly blessed life, a life distinguished by integrity, wisdom, military genius, and the remarkable fortitude he displayed upon the death of his son. I'd never deliberately ignore him, but I feel my heart leaping to . . .

[5] . . . Cato [*the Elder, Consul, second century BCE*]. The name and example set by that wisest of men calms my beating heart, like finding safe haven from a raging storm. That hero's exploits are legendary in war as well as politics, but I tend to admire them less than the fortitude he famously displayed in public upon the death of his son [*Licinianus*]—a Praetor Elect.

## RECENT EXAMPLES OF ROMAN FORTITUDE

[101] In absorbing Fortunes' heaviest blows uncomplainingly, some in our nation have bravely repeated these incredible examples of courage in the face of personal tragedy. It would not be difficult to add several here.

[6] When Quintus Marcius Rex [*Consul in 118 BCE*] lost his only son—a son of extraordinary

prudentiā pervicit et eo ipso die quo filii rogum spect-
aret, curiam ingressus est senatumque iussit convenire.

[*7*] Crassus, verò, in eo proelio quod cum Parthis com-
misit, occiso filio, tantum abfuit ut doleret ut etiam exer-
citum increpaverit, quòd unius militis iacturā tanto
opere commoveretur, hortatusque sit ut patriae virtutis
memores pro re publicā fortiter dimicarent, filii mortui
ultionem sibi uni relinquerent.

[*8*] [102] Sed antiquior P. Crassus, vir clarus et consul-
aris, P. Crassi filii mortem et vidit et moderatissime tulit.

[*9*] Nec ab eius laude abfuit—ac fortasse Crasso prae-
stitit—Cn. Caepio, qui Caepionem filium naufragio ab-
sumptum ita non doluit ut eum ne leviter quidem e vultu
aut ullā corporis parte commotum e familiaribus quisquam ullo pacto senserit.

[*10–16*] Iam ¿quid Pisones, Scaevolas, Brutos, Marcel-
los, Metellos, Lepidos, Aufidios enumerem? quorum
singuli pluribus amissis filiis vel uxoribus vel parentibus
nec lugendum existimarunt et suam in illorum funeribus

devotion and promise—he overpowered grief with discipline. The very day he watched his son be cremated, he walked into the Curia and called the Senate to order.

[7] [*Marcus Licinius*] Crassus [*Consul in 70 and 56 BCE*] saw his son killed in the battle he fought against the Parthians. He was so far from grieving, however, that he shouted at the army for getting so upset at losing a single soldier. "Remember your ancestors' valor, and fight bravely for our country!" he urged them. "And leave the job of avenging my son to me."

[8] [102] A more ancient Publius Crassus was a senator and sometime Consul [*see Letters to Atticus 12.24*]. He too witnessed his son, Publius Crassus, die, and took it in great stride.

[9] Equally impressive—and possibly surpassing Crassus—was Gnaeus [*Servilius*] Caepio [*Consul 55 BCE*]. Having lost his son, Caepio, in a shipwreck, he was so far from grieving that not a single friend could tell from his face or body that he was even marginally affected.

[*10–16*] Why list all the Pisos, the Scaevolas, Brutuses, Marcelluses, Metelluses, Lepiduses, the Aufidiuses? After losing many children or wives or parents, each thought grieving inappropriate. They believed a display of manful courage at those funerals

virtutem atque constantiam non sibi solum, sed etiam generi nominique Romano gloriosam fore putaverunt.

[103] Pudet in virorum gravissimis casibus repetendis longiori uti oratione, quum virorum maxime peculiaris virtus sit et in viris efflorescat ac vigeat maxime. Quamobrem, de feminis potius dicendum est ut, quum eas
fortissimas fuisse cognitum sit, tum pudeat viros a mulierculis virtutis exempla petere, et ab iis eā virtute in
quae ipsorum propria esse debeat, videri aliquando su-
peratos. [104] Nam si verum est, quod a Theophrasto
alicubi proditum memoriae mandavimus,

> "Orbem terrarum theatrum quoddam esse
> magnum divinā mente repletum et caelestis
> indicandae sapientiae gratiā tam multis undique
> collucentibus ornamentis illustratum ac depic-
> tum; in eo autem medio collocatos esse homines
> a deo, ut cum fortunā, dolore, morbis, egestate
> casibusque permultis adsidue luctentur; deum
> verò ipsum, quantùm quisque pugnando valeat,
> quàmque viriliter fortitudine divinitus acceptā
> utatur, desuper aspectare."

Hoc, inquam, si verum est, dubitari profectò non potest
quin,

would dignify not only themselves, but their families and the Roman name as well.

## ON MANFULNESS IN WOMEN

[103] It's embarrassing to go on rehearsing men's tragedies, because manfulness is literally a trait of men; it's mainly found and thrives in men. I ought to speak of *women* instead. Once we see that they've displayed incredible fortitude too, men will be embarrassed to have females as their examples of manfulness—and to realize that women have sometimes outdone them in the one strength that's supposed to be their own domain. [104] I mean, if it's true (as I believe Theophrastus states somewhere) that:

> "The cosmos is an immense 'theater' filled with Divine Intelligence and spangled and frescoed with starlight to convey the celestial wisdom. In the center, God set humans, in order to grapple constantly with misfortune, pain, sickness, poverty, and endless tragedies. Moreover, God himself is watching from above to see how each of us is sustaining the struggle and how manfully we're using the fortitude God has given us."[20]

If that's true, I say, then the implication is beyond doubt:

- quemadmodum populus Romanus in muneribus publicis invisos habet gladiatores, qui omni modo vitam impetrare cupiunt, favet iis qui contemptum eius prae se ferunt,
- itidem di immortales, si quos ex hominibus nimis anxie de vitā sollicitos eiusque exitum detrectantes aspiciant, iis aliquo modo suscenseant, eos verò et caros habeant et muneribus prosequantur qui, si e vitā revocentur ipsi vel suos revocari videant, alacres laetique deo pareant nihilque propterea mali sibi accidisse iudicent.

[105] Quod si feminas praestitisse intellegimus, ¿cur iis imbecilliores atque infirmiores videri velint viri? Neque solum unam aliquam e multis feminam, sed totam gentem ac nationem ut marium virtute sic feminarum eximiā quādam magnitudine animi praestitisse accepimus.

[106] Lacaenas enim matronas traditum est occisis filiis vulnera inspicere consuevisse, ac, si adversos vulneratos esse comperissent, laetabundas funus ducere eosque in avita sepulcra inferre solitas esse; contra verò, quos aversis vulneribus concisos agnoscebant, ab iis refugientes clam sepeliendos curabant nec ullo prorsus honore

- As Roman audiences jeer a gladiator in the arena who's too quick to beg and plead for life, and cheer for one that displays open contempt for it,
- So the immortal gods, if they see people frantic about life ending and refusing to leave, get in some way indignant at them. On the other hand, they cherish and bless those who, finding themselves or their loved ones being recalled from life, obey God cheerfully and happily, and don't decide that something bad is happening to them because of it.

[105] Moreover, if we learn that *women* have shown heroism, why would *men* be okay with looking more emotional and weak-minded than them? And it's not just a single woman we're talking about, but an entire *nation* whose women are as renowned for greatness of soul as the men are for prowess.

### Examples of Women in Sparta

[106] You see, we're told that in Sparta, when sons were killed in battle, their mothers would check the wounds. If they found the wounds in front, they'd lead the funeral processions joyfully and bury their children in the tombs of their ancestors. Conversely, if they found they'd been wounded from behind, they would turn away, have them buried in secret, and forbid that they be given any funeral service at

funeris prosequendos statuebant. Tantum in femineis quoque animis decus poterat et studium gloriae.

[107] Quā ex gente, etiam illud ad nos praeclarum dimanavit, matrem quandam filium sēnis confossum vulneribus intuentem nec ingemere voluisse nec coronam e capite deponere, sed ad comites conversam ita locutam:

> "¡Quanto pulchrius et optabilius est in acie
> victorem animam efflare quàm in Olympio
> certamine partā victoriā vivere!"

At alia, filium in proelio interfectum audiens,

> "Idcirco (*inquit*) genueram ut mortem pro patriā
> fortiter occumbere non dubitaret."

[108] ¿Quid his feminis facias, aut quo non honore ac gratulatione dignas putes quae de patriae dignitate deque gloriā sollicitae honestam mortem cuivis saluti ac lucro anteponerent?

Age verò, ¿num Lacaenis Romanarum virtus inferior? Par fortasse, nisi mālis etiam superiorem appellare.

all. *That's* how powerful a sense of honor and glory is, even in the hearts of women.

[107] Sparta also yields us this next inspiring report of a mother examining her son. He'd been fatally stabbed six times, but she refused to groan or remove the garland from her head. Instead, she turned to those around her and said,

> "It is far more glorious and desirable to win on the battlefield, and expire, than to win in the Olympics and live!"

Another, hearing her son had been killed in combat, said,

> "*This* is what I brought him into the world for: to meet death bravely, without hesitation, for his country."

[108] What can we say? These women were concerned for the dignity and glory of their country, so they preferred an honorable death to a life of comfort at any cost. What honor or congratulations do they *not* deserve?

### Examples of Women in Rome

And come *on*: are *Roman* women *less* courageous than Spartans? Equal, maybe—or maybe even more.

[1] ¡Quàm fortis enim et quàm magnifica illa Corneliae vox, quae duodecimo iam fetu amisso, quum Tiberium et Gaium filios interfectos spectavisset, nullo timore perculsa nulloque dolore confecta!

"Numquam (*inquit*) ego me non felicem dixerim,
quae Gracchos pepererim."

¡Fortem verò feminam et cuivis ex veteribus, mentis praestantiā ac magnitudine animi conferendam! Non enim dolori concessit, sed potius, quum virtute vicisset, victrix de dolore triumphum egit.

[2] [109] Nihil iam Rutiliam miremur, quae C. Cottam filium in exsilium secuta, quum postea reversum in patriam amisisset, nemo eam lacrimantem post elatum funus vidit.

[3] Parique fato Clodia usa est, quae D. Brutum filium consularem mortuum superstes vidit neque tamen eius obitum non fortiter et patienti animo tulit.

Quae virtutis non vulgaria in feminis exempla, mirari aliquis possit, qui sexūs imbecillitatem ac mollitiem cogitet. At verò, qui fortissimis genitas parentibus et fortibus etiam avis maioribusque prognatas recordatus fuerit, nihilo ab eis minorem vel prudentiam vel animi magnitudinem requirat.

[*1*] Consider that brave and glorious remark of Cornelia's. She'd already lost twelve children when she saw her sons Tiberius and Gaius assassinated. Instead of getting paralyzed by fear or traumatized by grief, she said,

> "I would never call myself unhappy: *I* bore the Gracchi!"

What a *heroic* woman! Her fortitude and greatness of soul equal any of the ancients! *She* did not wallow in grief, no; she *conquered* grief, manfully, and then *celebrated* her conquest in triumph.

[*2*] [109] So, let's no longer be surprised at Rutilia, who went with her son Gaius Cotta into exile and lost him once back. Nobody saw her shed a tear after the burial.

[*3*] It was the same with Clodia. She survived the death of her son Decimus Brutus—a former Consul [*in 77 BCE*]—yet endured his passing courageously and without complaint.

These extraordinary examples of manfulness in women might surprise you if you focus on the weakness and emotionality of the female sex. Remembering, though, that these women were scions of parents, grandparents, and ancestors of the greatest fortitude, you'd expect no less discipline or greatness of soul from them.

[110] ¿Est, ergo, ulla res tanti aut commodum ullum tam expetendum ut, illo amisso, ne prudentiam quidem retineamus?

Quae si ulla in nobis residet, nos profectò vel avitae vel patriae virtutis admonet, nec de Pisonibus, Fabiis, Brutis, Marcellis cogitantes quos imitemur et a quibus ortum ducamus immemores esse patitur. [111] Horum enim armis imperii fines producti sunt, horum sanguine parta ac stabilita libertas, horum denique labore ac studio res publica ad tantam pervenit sive bellicae laudis sive domesticae virtutis gloriam. Quorum in vestigia pedem ponere oportet, qui laudabiliter vivere quique honestis in actionibus exerceri volunt nec ullo mentis errore ad nimium dolorem atque insaniam traduci.

Nominavimus externos magnos clarosque viros; collegimus de nostris plurimos quibus mortis sensus non modo non ingratus, sed etiam optatus et iucundus accidit. Addatur, si placet, etiam Theramenes, qui—veneno epoto—maximā aequitate animi ludens in morte,

"quod erat in poculo reliquum,"

## IN SUMMARY: MAINTAIN ROMAN DISCIPLINE

[110] So: is any object so precious, or any privilege so enviable, that losing it should make us lose our heads, too?

If insight hasn't given up on us just yet, it surely reminds us of the greatness of our progenitors. It won't let us forget the Pisos, Fabiuses, Brutuses, the Marcelluses we descend from and should live up to. [111] You see, *their* armies extended our empire's borders, of *their* blood our freedom was born and strengthened, *their* toil and commitment elevated our country to its current peak of glory in both war and civilian life. If you want to live respected, live a life of honor, and avoid mistakes that lead to enormous grief and a nervous breakdown, *theirs* are the footsteps you should follow in.

## A CODA FROM ATHENS

I've cited the cases of great and famous foreign men, and I've collected a good many Romans who found dying not only *not* unpleasant, but even desirable and welcome. Let's add Theramenes [*of Athens, executed by order of Critias*], if you like. He chugged the poison, and fading away, deadpanned,

"Critias darling, *cheers!* I toast these last drops to you."[21]

Critiae propinavit. [112] Ergo, ille in suā morte vir clarus et sapiens ludebat; ¿nos in filiorum aut adfinium morte lugebimus? et veterum dicta cotidie legentes atque addiscentes praeclara ducemus, exempla repudiabimus? aut eam vitam quae mortem hanc consecutura est, immortalem, beatam, a miseriis omnibus vacuam negligemus? Quamvis enim nudum corpus et exanime discedens relinquat animus, nec amplius liceat homini qui e vītā discedat suis opibus, bonis, divitiis perfrui—

♫ . . . *astante* (ut ille ait) *ope barbaricā, tectis caelatis, laqueatis* . . . ♫

—tamen multo maioribus et bonis et opibus, quae nulla vetustas absumet, nulla vis eripiet, piorum mentes adsidue potiuntur.

[113] Sed dimittamus et exempla clarorum hominum et illorum virtutis impressam historiis memoriam; veniamus ad id quod unusquisque sensu percipit, quantumque ex morte consequamur emolumenti ac commodi re ipsā factisque probemus. Ex qua docendi ac disputandi ratione, perspicue veritas elucescit, quidque hōc modo se habeat, vel illo, facile potest perspici.

[112] If that wise statesman joked about his *own* death, will we cry at the deaths of children or relatives? As we go along reading and memorizing the words of the ancients each day, will we admire their wisdom but not follow their lead? Just forget the eternal, happy, blissful life to come after our death?

I know the soul's departure leaves the body naked and lifeless. I know a dying man can no longer enjoy his wealth, his riches, his money—

> ♪ . . . *surrounded by outlandish wealth,*
> *gold-coffered ceilings, gorgeous plasterwork* . . . ♪

—as the poet says. Yet by dying, good souls come into eternally *greater* riches—riches that no passage of time can ever diminish, nor any violence steal away.

[113] But let's forget about examples of famous individuals and the heroic record of greatness they stamped on history. Let's get down to things we *all* go through and use facts and real-world experience to try to quantify the benefits we reap from death. That approach to teaching and discussion best illuminates the truth and lets us see things as they really are.

[114] Si quisquam est qui secundos in omni vitā rerum exitūs adipisci et consequi possit nihilque timeat adversi,
hunc nemo infitiari poterit iure dicturum, si vitam sibi
morte multis partibus meliorem adfirmet. Atqui nemo est
qui non modo miserias atque aerumnas ab humanā vitā
segregare, sed ne semihoram quidem felicem sibi ac beatam polliceri possit.

[115] Metelli sibi fortunam sperant omnes; Priami
sobolem ac regnum exoptant alii.

- ¡Quasi non et Metellus tam multos nactus filios ac
  nepotes—quum maxime beatus esse posset—invitus
  obierit, et
- Priamum non omni orbatum progenie summoque
  dolore confectum hostilis manus interemerit!

His vitam si mors aliquot ante annis ademisset, e multis
eos miseriis ac luctibus simul eripuisset; quos idcirco experti sunt, quia vitam diutius quàm ipsorum requirebat
felicitas produxerunt. [116] Hinc illa miserabiliter
decantata:

126

## Timely Death Spares Us Grief

[114] If a person could theoretically succeed at everything all life long and never have to worry, they'd undeniably be right to say that in many respects, life is better than death. But so far from quarantining heartache and misery off from human life, there's not a person in the world who could guarantee him- or herself even half an hour of pure happiness!

[115] Everyone dreams of getting Metellus's life, while some fantasize about Priam's progeny and kingdom. Pfft!

- As if Metellus [*Macedonicus, Consul in 143 BCE*] *didn't* go unwillingly, although seeing all his many children and grandchildren could have brought him to the peak of happiness, and
- As if Priam [*legendary King of Troy*] *didn't* end up bereft of all his children, paralyzed by extreme grief, and killed by an invading army!

Had death claimed their lives a few years sooner, it would've spared them a great deal of misery and grief. Instead, they suffered precisely *because* they prolonged life longer than happiness required. [116] Hence that heartbreaking aria:

♫*Haec omnia vidi inflammari,*
*Priamo vi vitam auferri,*
*Iovis aram sanguine turpari.*♫

Quae non modo visu, sed etiam auditu acerbissima sunt. ¿Quid putamus misero regi qui omnia et videre et audire et experiri coactus est? ¿Num ei multo melius evenisset, si vitam omnino multis ante annis quàm haec acciderent amisisset? Forsitan quispiam dixerit: "Multa, quae vivens nactus est, bona citò decedens penitus reliquisset." Sed a malis etiam multo gravioribus, qualia multa saecula non viderunt, felicissime liberatus esset.

[117] Ex quibus omnibus multisque aliis, perspicuum est pervertere homines ea quae sunt humanae fundamenta felicitatis, quum utilitatem a morte seiungunt aut quum miseriam cum morte connectunt.

[118] L. Crassum, ex nostrā civitate clarissimum et eloquentissimum virum, matura mors ¡quantis e molestiis quantisque incommodis eripuit! Nam, qua in patriam pietate fuit, ex iis malis quae mortem eius consecuta sunt, incredibilem, si vixisset, dolorem accepisset. [119] Flagravit enim bello Italia, exarsit senatus invidiā, nihil denique in civitate fuit quod non eius temporis calamitatem luctumque persenserit. Nam ¿quid fugam Marii,

♪*I watched the flames engulfing all of this,*
*I saw the knife steal Priam's life,*
*and Jupiter's altar spattered with the blood.*♪

It's stomach-churning just to *hear* that, much less *watch* it; can you imagine the poor king that had to watch and hear and *live* it? Wouldn't a far better fate have been to simply lose his life years before that all happened? "By dying sooner, he'd have forever lost out on many blessings he enjoyed in life." I guess you could say that, yes, but he'd also have been mercifully spared the far greater horrors that many centuries haven't seen.

[117] These and many other examples prove that human beings skew the fundamentals of human happiness when they divorce expediency from death or link death to misery.

## THE LUCK OF CRASSUS

[118] Think of the heartache and headaches a timely death spared Lucius [*Licinius*] Crassus [*Consul in 95 BCE*], the finest orator in our country! Given his patriotism, if he'd lived, he'd have been grief-stricken beyond imagining at the horrors that followed his death [*in 91 BCE*]: [119] Italy erupting in war [*the Social War of 91–87 BCE*], the Senate a crucible of paranoia, not a thing in the country left untouched by the tragedy or grief of that era—the

quid cetera quae in illius discessu acciderunt maxime luc-
tuosa summeque miseranda commemorem? quid redi-
tum illum sanguinarium, cuius ex recordatione nemo est
qui non intimis sensibus exhorrescat? [120] Tenemus
enim memoriā, aut saltem ex patrum scriptis accepimus,
crudelissimam omnium caedem illo tempore esse factam,
trucidatos bonos viros et cives, incisas eorum cervices, in
Rostrisque positas, qui multorum civium salutem ac dig-
nitatem eloquentiā peperissent. ¡Quàm multos ex illā rei
publicae tempestate commemorare possumus, innocen-
tissimos homines atque optimos ut acerbissimam calamitatem effugerent, libertatem morte quaesisse!

[121] ¡O acerbum ac nemini non poenitendum rei publicae statum condicionemque vivendi! quum eos ipsos
qui rem publicam suo labore suoque sanguine auxerint,
iuverint, servarint, nusquam tutò nihilque magis quàm
propinquorum manūs ac gladios timentes horrescen-
tesque videas; illorum autem, quorum ope atque auxilio
servatus sis, quum horribiles miserosque casūs spectes,
nullā tamen ratione opitulari nihilque adferre adiumenti
queas. [122] ¿Quis neget iis ipsis qui haec intueri cogantur, mortem esse non modo <non> detrectandam, sed
etiam optandam?

Qui autem, ne in horum temporum flammam incidant,
mortis beneficio consecuti sint, eos verò beatissimos iure
omnes existimabunt; qualem fuisse L. Crassum, nisi res

flight and exile of [*Gaius*] Marius, the ordeals and horror stories his departure unleashed, the blood-bath his return became: why go into it all? It gives shudders to anyone who thinks back on it, [120] because we remember, or at least read in our fathers' books, that an indiscriminate bloodbath was perpetrated in that period. Good, patriotic heroes were massacred, and those whose eloquence had *created* the welfare and dignity of many citizens found themselves decapitated, their heads hung up for display in the Forum.[22] I can recall *so* many from that stormy period in our country's history—perfectly innocent, outstanding people—who sought freedom in death to escape that hideous nightmare!

[121] What a deplorable state for our country, what an abominable way to live!—where you see the very men whose blood and toil built, aided, and preserved our country nowhere safe, where their greatest fear and dread are the hands and swords of neighbors, and where you witness the gruesome and tragic fate of those whose help and aid saved your life, but you can't say or do anything to help. [122] Who would deny that for those who were forced to witness these sights, death was not only *not* to be refused, but even desired?

By contrast, we really can consider truly blessed those who were spared destruction in that holocaust by a natural death. Lucius Crassus was such

ipsa probavisset, nihil esset cur oratione persuadendum
videretur.

Sed haec paulo antiquiora quàm ut omnibus in memoriam
redigi ac cogitatione comprehendi possint. [123] Pompeii
autem, nostri familiaris, casu ¿quid in civitate notius, ¿quid
illustrius, aut ¿quid omnium oculis ac mentibus perspectius
et clarius? Hunc, si mature exstinctus esset, nihil doloris,
nihil invasisset mali. Quod tam diu in vitā mansit, idcirco
factum est ut singularis calamitatis exemplum omnibus
praebuerit. Cui eo luctuosior fortunae acerbitas visa est,
quo feliciore ac secundiore fortunā in omni vitā usus erat.
¿Quis enim universis civibus aliquando carior, ¿quis in togā
vel rebus gestis vel honoribus extra ordinem delatis clarior,
¿quis opibus, propinquitatibus, amicitiis florentior? cui
nihil prorsus ad summam absolutamque felicitatem praeter
honestum ac iucundum vitae exitum deesset.

[124] Sed, ¡videamus quantum in rebus humanis fortunae possit iniuria! (—Nisi malimus ad propriam mortalis vitae nimis asperam miseramque condicionem omnia
mala revocare.) Qui enim amplissimis fortunis usus erat,
qui nihil nisi sublime ac beatum nec cogitare nec optare
consueverat, cui omnia vel ad usum vel ad voluptatem

a man. If reality itself hadn't proven it, it'd be pointless to try to convince anyone of it in a speech.

### THE MISFORTUNE OF POMPEY THE GREAT

But those events all happened a little too long ago
for everyone to remember and internalize them.
[123] Pompey, though, my friend . . . nothing in
Roman history is more famous, no object lesson
more striking or blindingly obvious, than his down-
fall [*in 48 BCE*]. A timely death would've shielded
him from all heartache, all evil; staying *alive* so long
is what made him into a tragic figure like no other.
And in light of the happier and more prosperous
fortune he'd met with all his life, he found Fortune's
bitter irony all the more grievous. No one's ever
been more universally loved, never was anyone
more distinguished in politics for special appoint-
ments or achievements, never more blessed with
wealth, friendships, influence. His supreme and
perfect happiness lacked for absolutely nothing—
except an honorable and pleasant end of life.

[124] But *behold* the havoc Fortune can wreak in
human affairs! (Unless, that is, we'd rather blame
*all* our ills on the grueling condition of mortal life.)
You see, the same Pompey that commanded the
greatest fortunes, that contemplated or aspired to
nothing but the sublime and edifying, that had
everything you could ever need or want: *that* man

supererant, bellum cum socero suscepit, deseruit domum, profugit ex Italiā, et quum antea nihil in ceteris bellis nisi summo consilio prudentiāque gessisset, quum vel maxime ingenio iudicioque excellere debuisset, sui paene oblitus est. [125] Itaque, imbelles et infirmas copias—tirones collecticiosque milites—cum robustissimis legionibus conferre non dubitavit, et, amisso exercitu ereptisque castris, turpissime victus in servorum manūs vir summus et clarissimus incidit.

Vitā verò ut miserabiliter privatus sit, commemorare nihil est necesse, quum eo ipso—quòd in tam miseram fortunam delapsus vitam citò amiserit—minus fortasse miser censeri possit. Beatissimus autem obisset, si— quum in re publicā florebat, quum valebat auctoritate et gratiā, quum copiis opibusque adfluebat—e vitā decessis- set. Cuius propagatio quantum illi maeroris ac luctūs at- tulerit non modo scribendo, sed vix etiam cogitando, <haud> consequi quisquam possit.

[126] Itaque, hōc stabilito et fixo—mortem saepissime beatam homini contingere, non solum quòd nos in bea- tam vitam inducat, sed etiam quòd multarum magnarum- que miseriarum sensu liberet et a futuris vel calamitatibus

went to war against his father-in-law [*Julius Caesar*], abandoned his home, fled Italy. And, though in every other war he'd only taken action after careful planning and calculation, at the very moment he *should* have distinguished himself by his *greatest* strategic genius, he all but forgot himself. [125] He unthinkingly sent weak and untrained "troops"—raw, random recruits—into combat against battle-hardened infantrymen, and then—his army lost, camp plundered, himself defeated in disgrace—the great hero fell into the hands of . . . slaves.

There's no need to repeat the tragedy of his murder, since on that score—that after plummeting so low, he lost his life quickly—he could arguably be accounted *less* miserable. Either way, he would've died supremely happy if he'd departed life as the political darling he once was, at the height of his authority and influence, commanding soldiers and resources. It's impossible to describe or even *imagine* how much heartache and grief prolonging his life brought him.

## IN SUM: WE SHOULD WELCOME DEATH

[126] We've now determined that in numerous cases, death turns out happy. Not only does it usher us into a happy life, it also frees us from our endless stresses and rescues us from heartaches and

vel doloribus abstrahat—¿quid iam relinquetur cur non morte laetari ac clarorum hominum virtutem, qui nullius interitu perturbati sunt, imitari debeamus?

- ¿An non optimam beatamque mortem iudicabat L. Brutus, quum tyrannum arcens quem expulerat, vitam pro nihilo ducebat?
- Item Decii, quo tempore cum Latinis pro patriā dimicantes sese hostium telis obiiciebant?
- Praeterea Scipio, Paullus, Marcellus, Albinus, quos vitam in acie iuvandae patriae causā fortissime profudisse memoriae proditum legimus.

Et verò nihil fuit quamobrem, elato excelsoque animo homines vitam non despicerent ut sempiternam gloriam consequi possent. Nam cum nullo vel certe minimo doloris sensu, quem morientes perferunt, infinitam laudem commutabant.

[127] Hunc enim locum de exiguo vel nullo potius dolore mortis, quem supra perstrinximus, paulo uberius percurramus.

tragedies to come. So, what's to stop us now from *welcoming* death, and following the heroic model of those who remained famously untroubled by anyone's death?

- Didn't Lucius Brutus decide death was happy and the greatest good when, in seeking to keep the tyrant he'd overthrown out of Rome [*in 509 BCE*], he regarded his life as nothing?
- Ditto the Deciuses. Didn't they sacrifice themselves to the speartips of the enemy Latins [*340, 295 BCE*] for their country?
- Likewise Scipio [*212*], Paullus [*216*], Marcellus [*208*], and Albinus [*215*]? History tells us all of them laid down their lives to aid their country in battle.

In fact, there was no reason for those lofty, towering souls *not* to scorn life in order to win eternal glory, since they were trading the non-existent, or surely not much more, feeling of pain that the dying experience for infinite praise.

[127] I realize I gave that point—that death is painless or virtually so—short shrift earlier [*section 47*], so let's consider it a little more carefully.

Neque enim absurde dixisse mihi videtur is, qui morientium mortuorumque hominum statum et condicionem duabus potissimum ex rebus percipi atque intellegi posse adfirmavit, quarum unam somnum statuit, alteram verò tempus illud quod nostrum cuiusque ortum antecessit. [128] Et sane ita est ut, ex omnibus opinionibus quarum errore duci vulgus solet quum de morte loquitur, nulla plane ad veritatem videatur esse propensior. Ita enim multi vivunt ut praesentibus bonis fruantur nec sane cogitent quid paucis post annis vel ipsis vel ceteris boni aut mali possit evenire. Itaque, saepe non opinatis morbis, perturbationibus, angoribus vexantur; mortis verò, de qua potissimum cogitare debuerant, ita non reminiscuntur, ut ad se minimum illam pertinere nec suā quidquam interesse existiment. [129] Qui, ut Panaetius Africanum dicere solitum tradit, ferociores equos domitoribus tradendos esse ut paulatim parēre seque mitiores ac molliores praebere incipiant, sic ipsi in gyrum fortitudinis ac patientiae reducendi sunt, ne, si mors imprudentes oppresserit, perterreantur planeque concidant.

[130] Sed nescioquomodo voluptate luxuque delinita hominum consuetudo de rectā maiorum vitā deflexit,

## Death Is Painless or Nearly So

### SLEEP IS A PICTURE OF DEATH

You see, I think the man was on to something who claimed we can gain particular insight into the state and condition of the dead and dying from two situations, one being sleep, the other the time before our birth. [128] And of all the ideas that most mislead the masses when they speak of death, this one surely seems the most probable, because most people live in the moment and really don't think about the good or bad that can happen to them or others a few years from now. The result is that when trauma, emotions, and depression hit unexpectedly, they often get overwhelmed. Meanwhile, they don't even spare a thought for death—which they should have planned for most—since they assume it's totally irrelevant and uninteresting. [129] They're like aggressive horses, which, Panaetius says Scipio Africanus used to say, should be handed over to trainers to gradually learn obedience and compliance. In the same way, these people themselves need to be put into a training ring of fortitude and endurance; that way, if death catches them unsuspectingly, they won't panic and fall apart.

[130] Addiction to pleasure has somehow seduced and warped people's behavior from the upright

eoque sensim delata est ut nihil minus quàm verum agnoscat, nec, quum aliquid agitur, rectum id necne sit, magno opere cogitet. Qua nulla maior pestis ac pernicies humanis rebus—valde iam labefactatis—potuit adferri.

Atqui, si in ullo homine, certe in his ipsis vulgare dictum et verum et acute cogitatum esse deprehenditur. [131] ¿Quid enim isti aliud agunt nisi totos dies per inertiam perdunt atque ita vivunt ut stertere potius quàm ullo pacto vivere videantur?

- Dormiens autem ut nihil sentit, nihil agit, nihil curat,
- sic mortuus quid agere, quid curare aut sentire possit, haud sane intellegas.

Itaque, in fabulis, quos di maxime adamarunt, eos, ne imminentem aliquam calamitatem sentire cogerentur si vigilassent, a dis immortalibus consopitos esse accepimus.

[132] Mortem igitur, si quidem somno similis est, singulis noctibus induimus, et, quum in somno sensus sit plane nullus, nullum etiam in morte futurum esse sensum verissime statuere debemus.

lives our ancestors led. It's gradually reached a point where truth is what people know least, and in contemplating a course of action, they don't consider its moral impact in earnest. And with humanity already seriously compromised, no virus more fatal or insidious than that could be introduced.

If there's any truth and accuracy to the popular saying [*"sleep is a picture of death"*], surely there is with these people. [131] I mean, they waste whole entire days sitting around, "living" in such a way you'd think they're snoring, not living in any meaningful sense:

- As the *sleeping* man perceives nothing, does nothing, and cares about nothing,
- So what the *dead* man can or could do, care about, or perceive, is hard to tell.

Accordingly, legends tell us the immortal gods put those they cherish most into a deep sleep to spare them some imminent disaster they'd have to witness if awake.

[132] If death really *is* similar to sleep, therefore, we've been trying it on every night. And since there's obviously no awareness in sleep, the likeliest scenario, we should decide, is that there'll be no awareness in death, either.

Quod ut sensu ipso plane percipitur, sic ne de altero quidem dubitari ullo pacto potest quin

- quales antequam oriremur fuimus,
- tales etiam mortui futuri simus.

Mors enim quemadmodum ad eum qui nondum ortus est, nihil pertinuit, sic ne ad eum quidem qui mortuus est ullā ratione pertinebit. Ad morientem, verò, vel nihil vel parum certe pertinet, siquidem tam angusto spatio tamque brevi curriculo coercetur ut, ne si velit quidem, vires suas nimium porrigere aut explicare possit.

[133] ¿Quae est igitur eorum oratio qui tantum in morte dolorem se timere atque expavescere dictitant? Quamquam, non sane video quomodo aliter facere possint. Qui enim mortem numquam experti sint—quam semel homo subiturus est—¿quomodo bona malane sit, vere sentire ac diiudicare possunt?

Morientes aiunt cruciari, angi, distorqueri—quod in nonnullis fortasse animadverti atque observari potuit. [134] In quo, tum isti aliquid dixisse videri possent si hoc ex ipso mortis sensu pendēret. Nam, si mors ipsa dolore suo corpus usque eo cruciaret atque angeret ut haec doloris ēdere indicia cogeretur, negari profectò non posset

And as the senses themselves demonstrate this first claim clearly, so we cannot doubt that in the second case,

- As we were before birth,
- So we'll be when dead.

You see, just as death means nothing to the man who isn't born yet, so it will mean nothing at all to the man who's dead. Even for the *dying* man death means nothing or little, since it's limited to such a short duration and such a narrow compass that it couldn't extend or expand its force even if it tried.

## THE SIGNS ARE AMBIGUOUS

[133] What's the point, then, of all the wailing from people that they're so horribly afraid of death? Though, I don't really see what choice they have. I mean, if you've never *experienced* death—and a human being will only undergo it once—how can you actually try it and decide whether it's good or bad?

"The dying," they say, "get tortured, strangled, and pulled apart in agony." Yes, it's possible we *have* seen signs of that in some cases. [134] And they'd possibly have a point on that score if the suffering were a function of the *feeling* of death. I mean, if death's painfulness itself *did* so torture and strangle the body that it were *forced* to manifest

143

quin dolorem non levissimum mors ipsa esset adlatura. Quum verò huius modi cruciatus paucissimos angat—et eos maxime qui intemperanter, flagitiose, nefarie vixerint—nunc dubitari non potest quin tales homines non mors, sed admissorum scelerum conscientia vexet habeatque sollicitos.

[135] Qui enim se morituros numquam crediderint ac ne cogitarint quidem, quum ad ipsam mortem pervenerint, anguntur non dolore moriendi, sed quòd e vitā inviti discedunt. In quā, quum omnia secunda feliciaque experirentur, ne secus mortuis accidat, valde vereri ac dubitare coguntur.

[136] At bonis, qui mortem semper tamquam praesentis tempestatis portum in ore ac sermone habuerint quique ex huius vitae procellis mortis beneficio aliquando egredi saepissime concupiverint, nihil libentius ac iucundius mentione ac nomine mortis accidit. Atque in iis etiam praestans planeque admirandum deorum munus agnoscitur. Bonos enim et quidem plurimos, non modo cum exiguo dolore ut optare homines vulgò solent, sed omnis plane doloris expertes ex hāc vitā egressos sine ullā dubitatione reperias. [137] Ex quibus,

those signs of pain, then case closed: death is going to really hurt. But because throes like that afflict very few, and primarily those who've lived immoderate, sinful, wicked lives, the reality can only be that the cause of their anguish and distress isn't death, but their guilty conscience.

[135] You see, when death comes to people who never believed they'd die—never even gave it a thought—what torments them isn't the pain of dying, but the fact that they're being forced to leave. They have to assume and worry that, because everything went so spectacularly in life, it'll be different in death.

## CASES OF SUDDEN DEATH SUGGEST PAINLESSNESS

[136] With people of *virtue*, it's different. To those who always spoke of death as a refuge from an unrelenting storm, and always craved the blessing of death to finally escape the fury of this life, nothing sounds sweeter or more delightful than the word *death*. Their experiences are an excellent illustration of how wonderful the gods' gift is, since it's easy to find a great many virtuous people who departed this world not only suffering very little—that's what we all hope for—but without any suffering at all. Examples include [137]:

- Q. Fabius, consulatum adeptus, quum in curiā praetereuntes salutaret—nihil dolens, nihil molesti sentiens, immo plane gaudens—e vitā discessit.

Atque idem contigit:

- Pompeio, quum in aede Iovis Capitolini sacra fecisset,
- itemque Thalnae consuli, dis immortalibus supplicanti.

¿Quid hos in ipso mortis articulo doloris expertos existimes, qui paulo ante laeti vivebant, et in eo quo moriebantur puncto temporis, nihil lugubre testati sint, nihil flebile dixerint? "Morte," inquies, "oppressi sunt." [138] At sapientissimi et optimi viri, quibus mortem tamquam beatae vitae initium di immortales largiri voluerunt; quam eo fortasse iucundiorem ipsis fore videbant, quo minus eo tempore tantum boni exspectaverant ac ne sperare quidem poterant. Nam quum mors e divinā voluntate tota pendeat, haud sane in hominis potestate esse possit quo potissimum die quāque condicione mori velit.

- Quintus Fabius [*Maximus*], who'd recently become Consul [*45 BCE*]. While shaking hands in the receiving line in the Senate building— without any pain, feeling nothing amiss, indeed, beaming—he dropped dead.

The same happened to:

- [*Aulus*] Pompeius [*Tribune, 102 BCE*], while leading Mass in the Temple of Capitoline Jupiter, and
- [*Manius Juventius*] Thalna, the Consul [*163 BCE*], while leading a public prayer of supplication.

What pain can you imagine they felt at the very instant of death? They were alive and happy moments before, and in the seconds it took to die, they showed no sign of suffering or complaint. "Death zapped them," you'll say. [138] No, it's *because* of their wisdom and greatness that the immortal gods chose to *reward* them with death, as an entrance to a happy life. The gods apparently figured that if those men had no reason to expect or hope for so great a blessing at that time, they'd find death all the more pleasant. Death depends entirely on the gods' will, you see, so the exact date and circumstances of dying are not of man's choosing.

[139] Nec verum est, quod dicitur a quibusdam, mortis eundem omnibus hominibus diem ac terminum divinitus esse constitutum; ut autem vel citius vel serius moriamur, singulorum hominum vel [in]temperantiā vel negligentiā contingere. Nam ut illud verissimum est praefinitum esse vitae terminum a deo quem praeterire aut ex quo egredi nemini liceat, sic illud adfirmare nemo possit, eundem omnibus eādemque horā vitae finem impendēre. [140] Quod si agnosceremus, nihil sane esset cur homini prudentiam, temperantiam, pietatem tribueremus. Quae omnes plane virtutes, si hoc consequeretur, non modo inutiles, sed penitus inanes viderentur.

¿Cur enim prudentiā uteretur homo, cur abstinentiā, cur temperantiā, si eodem quo reliqui omnes temporis spatio vitam esset terminaturus? "Ut diutius," inquis, "vitam producere liceret." [141] At, si vitae terminus fatalis est, ne immutari quidem posse necesse est. Sin voluntarius et in hominis arbitrio positus, nihil est cur eundem omnibus a deo constitutum esse quisquam adfirmet.

Sed de his statuat unusquisque ut libet. Quid autem verius sit, deus ipse viderit; hominem quidem scire arbitror neminem. Stet modo nobis illud, doloris esse nihil in morte, boni autem tantum ex eā ad homines permanare quantum sperare multi possint, cogitatione quidem adsequatur nemo. Itaque, hoc divinitus hominibus datum

## HUMANS HAVE NO FIXED LIFE SPAN

[139] It's also untrue, despite what some say, that the human species is programmed with the same divinely fixed expiration date, and that whether we die before or after it is determined by individuals' healthy or unhealthy choices. You see, as sure as it is that God has foreordained a limit to life that none of us can exceed or escape, it's equally certain that nobody could prove that the same type and hour of death await us all. [140] If we really thought it did, we'd have no reason to praise a person for maintaining discipline, making healthy choices, or being religious. From then on, all those virtues would seem not just useless, but utterly meaningless.

I mean, why practice risk avoidance, discipline, or make healthy choices if life is going to expire on the same timeline as everyone else? "To prolong life" you say. [141] But if life is term limited by fate, then, necessarily, you *can't* change it; whereas if the end *is* a matter of choice and up to us, there's no reason to claim God has fixed the same life span for us all.

Well, let's each decide that one for ourselves. God alone can figure the truer version out, since I don't think any *human* knows. Let's just agree that there's no pain in death, and that actually, it's the source of more good than many of us could hope or even imagine. It explains why humans have a God-given

est, ut quotiens molesti aliquid experiantur, tum mortem exoptent ac votis etiam conceptis saepe implorent. ¿Quid ita? quia bonam utilemque esse mortem coguntur agnoscere; malam autem aut acerbam esse numquam posse, homini a naturā insitum est. [142] Itaque, dolore perculsi mortem imploramus eamque unam ut miseriarum malorumque terminum exoptamus.

Admonet me locus ut, quum neminem ipsā morte magno opere commoveri debere probatum sit, iis praecipue dolendum nihil esse contendam quos mors cum laude oppetita consolari potest. Satis enim diu vixisse putandi sunt, qui vitam honeste clauserunt. Eosdemque e vitā abeuntes non modo laus, sed etiam perpetua voluptas delectatioque prosequitur. Quae sane eo maior in animo exoriri ac vigere solet, quo latior alicuius in colendo officio vitāque honeste ducendā manavit industria. [143] Certe enim, quum ad recte agendum natus homo sit, ideoque mentis et rationis munere prae ceteris animantibus ornatus atque instructus, ¿unde potius laudem ac voluptatem quàm ab honestis actionibus petat? ¿An unde ortum duxerit, obliviscatur?

Ille, verò, nec sui oblitus est qui recte vixit, nec iniquo animo mori potest, quum multos relinquat suae testes memoresque virtutis.

habit of wishing for death every time they suffer a setback; they often even swear to God they want it. Why? Because they're hit with the realization that death is good and expedient, and Nature has planted the instinct in humans that death can never be evil or hurtful. [142] Accordingly, in moments of despair we cry out for death, asking for it alone to terminate our suffering.

## A GLORIOUS DEATH MAKES GRIEF UNNECESSARY

On that note: Now that we've proven death per se shouldn't really upset anyone, I should demonstrate that grief is especially unnecessary when you can take comfort in a *glorious* death. You see, a life must be considered sufficiently long when it's concluded with honor; it goes out in triumph and finds everlasting bliss in its train. Moreover, the harder you've worked to fulfill your duties and live a life of honor, the greater that feeling grows and intensifies in your soul. [143] I mean, man was surely born to do good; that's *why* we're graced with an intellect superior to all other animals. Where else, then, should we seek greater glory or satisfaction than in honorable conduct? Should we *forget* our origins?

Well, live a moral life and you'll show you *didn't* forget. You'll also die without regret, since you'll be leaving behind so many witnesses to your integrity.

[144] ¡Quanto autem gaudio exsultare credendus est illorum animus, qui corporis admixtione solutus in caelestes ignes sempiternasque domos, unde exierat, revertit!

Profectò enim ex divinā mente delibatos habemus animos, qui hac mole inclusi, tamquam <corpus> terrae gravitate, sic ipsi nimio pondere corporis opprimuntur. Ubi autem soluti corporibus ad proprias sedes evolaverunt, tum vere vivunt nec libidini, voluptati, dolori serviunt, sed sui compotes nullā re anguntur, nihil requirunt, omnibus imperant. [145] Recte igitur dictum est

"corpus terram esse, mentem autem ignem de caelo sumptum"

—id quod clarorum virorum acta cum virtute vita, praeclaraeque actiones, facile testantur. ¿Quomodo enim aut

- omnia humanae vitae commoda contemneret, aut
- voluptates cunctas pro nihilo duceret, aut
- vitam ipsam laudis honestatisque gratiā profunderet,

# The Human Soul Is Divine and Immortal

## THE HEAVENLY ORIGINS AND ASPIRATIONS
## OF THE SOUL

[144] Imagine the *thrill* such honorable souls must feel when they get free of their bodily adulteration and return home to the starry heavens and eternal dwellings they came from!

You see, we surely have souls sampled from a Divine Intelligence. Trapped in our molecules, they're held here by the oppressive weight of our bodies the same way gravity holds our bodies to earth. When they're released and fly back home where they belong, though, *real* life begins. Emancipated from desire, pleasure, and pain, they're autonomous at last: serene, independent, in absolute control. [145] I agree, therefore, that

"The body is earth, but the mind is fire from heaven."[23]

The proof lies in the heroic lives and grand gestures of great men. I mean, how could they:

- Turn their back on all that's good in this world, or
- Count every pleasure as nothing, or
- Sacrifice their very lives for honor and glory

qui nihil quidquam ad se praeter haec ipsa mortalia quae manibus contrectat, quae terit pedibus, pertinere cogitaret?

Verùm haec non ita se habent. Corpus enim e terrā concretum tam diu terrestrium rerum amore ducitur quoad in terram ipsam, unde ortum duxit, revertatur. Animus verò, qui e caelo sumptus est, sempiternum quiddam et caeleste appetit nec iisdem quibus corpus finibus cogitationes coercet suas. Itaque, numquam quiescere nec vere vivere putandus est, quamdiu corpore conclusus invitus propemodum mortali labe terrenisque vinculis cohibetur.

[146] At illa ¡quanti sunt, gravissimis vitae laboribus liberari, in mediis doloribus et aerumnis obdormiscere et quasi emissos e molestissimā vitae custodiā in iucundissimam suavissimamque domum remigrare! Huc enim pertinent quae de piorum quiete, deque voluptate illā qua egressi e vitā perfrui dicuntur, disputari a sapientibus solent. Qui quum intellegerent non fortuitò aut temere satos et creatos homines esse, nec eadem mereri bonos, qui multis exanclatis laboribus vitam in medio dolore amisissent, et improbos, quorum in patrandis flagitiis semper est animus cogitatioque defixa, idcirco non eundem probis et improbis vitae terminum nec eadem mortuis praemia statuerunt.

if all that matters to them are these material things we touch and feel and step on?

But that isn't what happens. You see, the *body* is formed of earth, and it's forever spellbound by earthly things until it returns back into its mother earth. The *soul*, by contrast, is taken from heaven. It longs for something heavenly and eternal and doesn't restrict its thoughts to the same limits as the body. Hence it has, we must assume, no rest or real life as long as it remains trapped in the body, imprisoned in earth's shackles and mortal mire.

[146] Imagine the *relief*, though, of finding *freedom* from life's crippling toils, and *sleep* amidst suffering and pain! It's like getting released from a horrible prison—life—into a supremely happy and joyful home. *This* is what philosophers mean when they speak of the tranquility and joy we're told the righteous enjoy upon departing this world. They understood humans weren't created or put here at random or without design. They understood that *good* people who suffer enormously and then die tragically don't deserve the same fate as wicked people whose hearts and minds are forever fixated on committing crimes. Hence, they determined, the span of life is not the same for the good and the evil, and their rewards in death aren't the same, either.

[147] Qua nos recordatione potissimum refici ac recreari decet, qui carissimam filiam optimeque de nobis meritam ita vixisse scimus ut ad optimos mores summamque prudentiam nihil posset accedere, et ita mortuam ut in dolore quem ex partu contraxerat, summam animi magnitudinem summamque constantiam praestiterit.

Cuius mentio nobis—dolore iam, si non penitus exstincto, certe magno opere levato—non solum acerba sed etiam iucunda accidit. ¿Quî enim aliter debet? quum nec ipsi quidquam accideret mali nec ego ullā re quae tanto opere cum naturā congruat, et cum omnibus hominibus communicet, angi aut perturbari debeam. [148] ¿Quid ergo mihi restat? Nihil sane, nisi—quum ea divino potissimum beneficio vitae munere perfuncta sit—ut ad eam maxime vivendi condicionem cogitationem meam mentemque referam qua nunc ipsam perfrui credimus, ac—si, quod aequum est, fateri velimus—etiam intellegimus.

Qua ex meditatione, eo maiorem voluptatem percepturus sum quo meliore illa nunc statu, quàm quem vivens experta est, sine ullā dubitatione perfruitur. ¿Quid enim boni non merita est, quae nihil umquam egit ac ne cogitavit quidem mali, et iis angoribus ac malis quae viventi obiecta sunt, ita patienter perfuncta sit ut non secus de adversis quàm de secundis rebus dis immortalibus gratulari gratiasque agere soleret? et quum nihil nisi rectum

## TULLIA'S GREATNESS

[147] That realization should above all lift my own spirits as I think of my precious, wonderful daughter. She *lived* in such a way that her good nature and incredible discipline could not be bettered, and she *died* in such a way that even while suffering painful complications from childbirth, she exhibited awesome endurance and greatness of soul.

Remembering her, now that the pain is fading if not gone, doesn't just get me choked up anymore; it makes me smile, too. How could I not? Nothing bad can happen to *her*, and I myself shouldn't worry or get upset at anything so natural or universal a human experience. [148] So, now that, thanks to a special blessing of the gods, she's acquitted herself of her duty to life, what's next for me? Only this: to focus all my thoughts on the kind of existence that I believe—no, that I *know*—she's enjoying right now.

And *that* thought makes me smile all the more, since the state she's enjoying now is unquestionably better than what she got in life. I mean, what happiness is she *not* entitled to? She never *contemplated*, much less did, anything bad. And she put up with the challenges and problems life threw at her so uncomplainingly that she'd thank the immortal gods for her setbacks no less than her successes! She sought to do only what's good and right,

honestumque cogitaret, tamen unā conscientiā contenta nec sua benefacta in luce collocari nec sibi quidquam propterea laudis aut gloriae deberi arbitraretur. [149] Quae, ergo, ita animata fuerit ut de se quidem minimum, de rectā mente ac de aequitate plurimum laboraret, ¿an non dis ipsis censemus maxime gratam et probatam fuisse, in qua non ficta et adumbrata ut in multis, sed maxime solida et expressa virtutis elucebat effigies?

Nam, quum eam talem natura genuisset ut quod pulchrum rectumque agnoscebat suā sponte sequeretur, tamen eo non contenta, summā vi rationis prudentiaeque perfecerat ut nullā re minus quàm naturā duce egere videretur. [150] Itaque, qui eius instituta et mores paulo diligentius inspexisset, qui regundae familiae sollertiam, qui summum in cunctis rebus ingenium singularemque doctrinam advertisset, haud fuisset sane quod aut virilem in intellegendis iudicandisque rebus prudentiam aut exquisitam patrisfamilias sollertiam requireret.

Itaque, quibus maxime rebus egere saepe homines solemus, fortitudo et prudentia, hae ita in muliere abundabant ut sui maeroris medicinam non peteret foris, sed in se ipsam spectans ex suā semper virtute pendēret.

Quanto autem graviores ac difficiliores animi morbi sunt quàm corporis, eo magis mirandum est talem exstitisse illam, cuius fortitudini corporis mala parērent, prudentiae verò omnes animi morbi facile cederent.

but she was content to keep it to herself. She never thought to advertise her good works or expected any recognition for them. [149] With a heart bent entirely on justice and fairness and never on herself, then, *shouldn't* I think she found the greatest favor with the immortal gods themselves? In her, we saw the embodiment of greatness—not a flimsy imitation, as in many, but rock-solid, defined, and radiant.

You see, she was naturally predisposed to side with what she deemed noble and right, but she didn't stop there. She'd analyze and assess situations so masterfully you'd think native wits were the one thing she needed least. [150] And if you'd examined her conduct and character in greater detail, or witnessed her skillful household management, deep knowledge, and knack for everything, hardly anything would've needed a man's wisdom or patriarch's acumen to understand and settle matters.

She was a woman, and yet fortitude and practicality—so rare even in us men—were so highly developed in her that she never sought outside help for her ordeals. Instead, she'd look to *herself* and rely on her own inner strength.

Moreover, to the extent that emotional traumas are more serious and challenging than physical traumas, it's all the more impressive that she overcame her *physical* problems with fortitude, while she conquered every *emotional* trauma with practicality.

Itaque, quamquam ex calamitate temporibusque nostris molestiae plurimum traxerit, numquam tamen animo perculsam aut deiectam sensimus. [151] Angebatur patris exsilio, totiusque familiae luctum bonorumque direptionem invita videbat, sed matri tamen consilio prudentiāque aderat, et rebus in magnum saepe discrimen adductis, reditūs spem nobis adferre numquam dubitavit. Ita, quantum ex calamitate doloris, tantundem ex filiae suavitate ac pietate solacii capiebamus.

Quod ut esset diuturnius, si commodum nostrum aut eam, quae omnibus antiquissima est, liberorum caritatem cogitaremus, magno opere optare debuimus.

At, quum illam corporis vinculis solutam, omnibus exutam miseriis et immortalitatis compotem factam animo reputamus, non modo in dolore conquiescimus, sed etiam praecipue laetamur. [152] ¿Quid enim mihi accidere laetius potest quàm de immortalitate animorum cogitanti de filiae simul aeternā beatāque vitā confidere? Animos enim esse immortales ne dubitandum mihi quidem videtur.

Hence, even though she suffered enormously because of my own misfortunes [*in 58–57 BCE*], I never saw her flustered or depressed. [151] She *was* distraught at her father's exile; it hurt to see her whole family weeping and our property confiscated. But she was there for her mother, offering advice and perspective, and every time we were on the verge of a breakdown, she was adamant that I'd return. So, for all the grief my disaster gave us, our daughter's loving devotion equaled it in solace.

In fact, if all I cared about were myself or a father's instinctive love, I'd want that period to go on longer.

Realizing, though, that she's free of her body's shackles, past all suffering, and in possession of immortality, my pain doesn't just subside; it turns into great joy. [152] I mean, in reflecting on the immortality of souls, what could make me smile more than believing in my daughter's life of eternal happiness? Because souls *are* immortal, I think, and I don't think we can doubt it.

Faciam autem non invitus ut sapientissimorum hominum percurram hac de re sententiam, quando me in hunc locum deduxit oratio.

Neque verò haec ita disputanda censeo, ut animos idcirco non interire probari possit quòd mortuorum corporibus vis quaedam inesse veneratione digna putetur, quae significare debeat non deleri morte animos, sed immortalium animorum veluti sepulcra quaedam, mortalia corpora fuisse. Quasi non et maiora et firmiora multa suppetant quibus planum fieri possit, qui animos simul cum corporibus interire contendat, eum contra rationem nullā nixum ratione pugnare.

[153] Quod si auctoritas quaerenda sit, ¿quem graviorem nominare auctorem possum quàm eum quem Apollo ipse sapientissimum omnium pronuntiavit? Cuius testimonium tale fuit ut, divinos esse hominum animos et eos corpore solutos in caelum remigrare unde prius venissent, in omni sermone adseveraret.

162

## ARGUMENTS FOR THE IMMORTALITY
OF THE SOUL

Since this essay's led me to the point, I'll gladly review the greatest thinkers' thoughts on the immortality of the soul [*cf. section 4*].

### A Bad Argument: The Fact That People Visit Graves Proves Nothing

As a preliminary matter, I *don't* think we should try to prove souls don't perish on the basis that some people worship a kind of supernatural spirit which they believe remains in the bodies of the dead [e.g., *by visiting a grave; cf. 161–162 below*], and that rather than death wiping our souls out, this spirit allegedly proves mortal bodies were actually "tombs" for immortal souls. That would imply that many stronger arguments *aren't* available to show how those who maintain that souls and bodies perish together, are fighting logic illogically.

### Appeal to Authority: Socrates, Pythagoras

[153] If it's authorities we want, what more imposing authority can I cite than the man [*Socrates*] that Apollo himself declared wisest of all? His life's work was to assert at every turn that our souls are divine and that, freed of their bodies, they return to the heavens they came from.

In quo, cum philosophis illis consensit quos quondam "Italicos" nominavit antiquitas maximeque nobiles iudicavit, quorum semper constans fuit opinio demitti animos e caelo divinaeque mentis eos esse non solum munus, sed etiam partem praecipuam ac propriam.

Quod si secus esse quisquam putet, haud sane facile quid multis et firmissimis in hanc sententiam argumentis respondere possit, inveniet.

Sic enim plane cognosci ac sensu ipso diiudicari potest, summam esse paeneque incredibilem in animis celeritatem ac festinationem, cuius ope, quae corpus non modo certo mensium sed vix etiam annorum spatio perficere atque exsequi posset, ea ipsi non modo semel puncto temporis percurrere, sed etiam saepius excogitare et repetere facillime queant.

[154] Quod si mirum videtur, ¿cur non admirabilius censeatur meminisse animum tam multa innumerabilibus ante saeculis gesta, quae futura sunt cogitando prospicere ac non modo praesentia, sed etiam praeterita et futura veluti deum omnia complecti ac sub oculos subiicere conari?

¿Quis dubitet, quum haec intellegat eademque in se ipso agnoscat, divinum esse animum, nec—si divina aeterna sunt—ipsum esse mortalem?

On that point, he agreed with the renowned philosophers that antiquity once called "the Italians" [*Pythagoreans*]. Their unwavering view was that souls descend from heaven, and that they're not only a gift of the Divine Intelligence, but a special part of its essence [*cf. section 144*].

Anyone who disagrees with that view is going to have trouble finding ways to rebut the many strong arguments in its favor.

## "Magical" Properties of the Soul: Speed, Memory, Motion

For example, our senses alone can tell us souls possess an extreme, almost mind-boggling velocity and spontaneity. Tasks that would take our bodies months or even years to carry out and perfect, our minds can analyze, engineer, and iterate in an instant—and easily.

[154] If that seems weird, isn't it even *weirder* that the mind remembers so many events from countless ages past? That it predicts future outcomes? That, like a god, it seeks to comprehend in a single view not only the present, but the past and future as well?

When you think about this, when you recognize it in yourself, how could you doubt the soul is divine? And if what's divine is eternal, that the soul is immortal?

Quum praesertim duabus ex rebus, quae praecipuae in animo sunt, illius aeterna natura facile intellegi ac deprehendi possit. Haec autem sunt motūs qui in eo praecipuus est,

- principium, ac
- perpetuitas.

Quum enim ex se ipso moveatur nec aliunde, ut cetera, principium motūs mutuetur;

summa autem in eo, quamdiu in corpore est, perpetuitas motūs appareat—quippe quae etiam in dormientibus agnoscatur et vigeat—idcirco dubitari nullo modo potest quin divinus sit et sempiternus futurus. [155] Et sane ita esse, ratio vincit et rerum probat exitus.

Dei enim imago quaedam animus est ex ipso deo delibata ac profecta. Quod si deus immortalitate fruitur, ¿cur eam partem quam ex se ipso sumpsit mortalem esse velit?

Quin hōc ipso singularem et eximiam divinam esse vim indicandum putavit, quòd non solum ipse immortalis sit, sed etiam quos velit suae naturae compotes et plane immortales, efficiat.

Corpus autem voluit esse mortale, nec immeritò, quum e terrā—cuius mutationi subiecta natura est—initium duxerit, et in eam ipsam, vitae cursu confecto, abire debeat.

The soul's eternal nature can be even more easily grasped from its two characteristic properties:

- It *initiates* motion, and
- Its motion is *uninterrupted*.

You see, the soul moves *on its own*; unlike other things, it doesn't get set in motion by something else.

Moreover, the *uninterruptedness* of its motion is evident the whole time it's inside the body, inasmuch as it's active and observable even in people asleep. These facts prove beyond doubt that the soul is divine and will be everlasting. [155] Reason compels that conclusion, and reality confirms it.

You see, the soul is an image of God, sampled and emanating from God. Now, if God is immortal, why would He want the part He took from *Himself* to be mortal?

No, that's exactly *why* He felt obliged to hint that this strange, unparalleled power is divine: to show us He isn't just immortal Himself, but also *shares* His immortal nature with those He chooses.

The *body*, though, He *did* want mortal. And that makes sense, since it comes from the earth, whose nature is to change, and, when life's course is complete, into earth it must return.

Sed animus profectus a deo caelum ipsum appetit; nam in eum locum unde discessit, semper optat redire. Terra autem, si cui appetenda, corpori soli est. [156] At verò animis aeterna caeli sedes quaerenda eaque propria illorum patria, siquidem **animorum nulla in terris origo inveniri potest. Nihil enim est in animis mixtum atque concretum aut quod ex terrā natum atque fictum esse videatur, nihil ne aut humidum quidem aut flabile aut igneum. His enim in naturis nihil inest quod vim memoriae, mentis, cogitationis habeat, quod et praeterita teneat et futura praevideat et complecti possit praesentia. Quae sola divina sunt nec invenietur umquam unde ad hominem venire possint nisi a deo. [157] Singularis est, igitur, quaedam natura atque vis animi, seiuncta ab his usitatis notisque naturis. Ita, quidquid est illud quod sapit, quod vult, quod viget, caeleste et divinum est, ob eamque rem aeternum sit, necesse est. Nec, verò, deus ipse qui intellegitur a nobis alio modo intellegi potest nisi mens soluta quaedam et libera, segregata ab omni concretione mortali, omnia sentiens et movens ipsaque praedita motu sempiterno.**

## The Soul's Nature Cannot Be Paralleled on Earth

But the *soul*, having emanated from God, seeks the heavens themselves, for it forever longs to return to the place it came from. If anything gravitates toward the *earth*, it's the body. [156] *Souls* must seek the eternal abode of the heavens, their true homeland, since the origin of souls is not to be found on earth. You see, there's nothing blended or amalgamated in souls, or anything that looks to be formed or made of earth. There's not even anything humid, or airy, or fiery, since there's nothing in natures of that kind which has the power of memory, understanding, or thought, and which can remember the past, foresee the future, and comprehend the present. Divinities alone have those capabilities, and no source will ever be discovered from which a person could get them, except God. [157] There is, therefore, a unique nature and power in the soul, distinct from those more known and familiar natures. Whatever "it" is, then, that reasons, that has volition, and that is alive, it is heavenly and divine, and hence must necessarily be eternal. Moreover, God Himself as we conceive of Him cannot be conceived of as anything other than a free and unencumbered Intelligence, devoid of all mortal elements, perceiving all, moving all, and itself endowed with

[*V21*] [158] Itaque, eandem aeternitatem animis quoque nostris ex se ipsā exortis impartivit. Quorum ex cogitationibus atque operibus, nihil aliud nisi divinos esse illos et sempiternos colligere possumus.

Nam,

- si aedificiorum magnitudinem atque ornatum,
- si monumenta litterarum,
- si pecuniae vim infinitam in res maxime stabiles et admirandas effusam,
- si plurimarum maximarumque rerum adeptionem cogitare voluerimus,

profectò intellegemus haec numquam facturum fuisse hominem, nisi diuturnitatem temporis ipsamque aeternitatem plurimum ad se pertinere existimaret. Iam ipsa gloriae cupiditas, honorum sitis, opum ac divitiarum adsidua procuratio: ¿quid aliud indicat nisi cogitare hominem in posterum nec eodem vescendi vivendique studio quo ceteras animantes duci videmus, humanum animum detineri?

Sed haec abiectiora atque humiliora, nec ullis—nisi sane angustis naturae terminis—circumscripta. [159] ¿Quid illa inprimis gravia atque praestantia nec ulli plane in terris

**perpetual motion.** [158] That Intelligence has shared that same eternity with our souls, which emanate from it; and from their thoughts and operations, we can infer that our souls can only be divine and eternal.

### The Appeal to Art

If we'll only ponder

- the grandeur of soaring architecture
- the masterpieces of literature
- the immense sums poured into monumental projects
- the fulfillment of so many grand ambitions

we'll *understand* that man would've *never* done those things if he didn't believe the eons of eternity *mattered* to him. The very desire for glory, the craving for honor, the blind striving for wealth and resources: what do they show other than that man *does* think of tomorrow, that man's soul is obviously *not* confined to the same drives—eating, survival—as other animals?

### The Appeal to Science

But those pursuits are paltry and parochial, their scope narrowly confined to worldly interests. [159] What of those infinitely more sublime attributes—those

degenti nisi soli homini tributa? contemplatorem esse ipsum caeli rerumque caelestium, frui magnarum obscurissimarumque rerum scientiā quae vel ad excolendos ad integritatem atque innocentiam mores, vel ad comparandam solis astrorumque cognitionem, vel ad exercendam in abditis obscurisque rebus memoriam mentemque pertineant. [160] ¿Nonne haec ipsa tanta ac talia divinum esse animum ostendunt, nec illius naturam aliunde quàm e caelo delibatam ac deductam?

¿An censemus—si unā cum corporibus animi interirent—aut sapientissimos homines tam aequo animo mori posse aut tam iniquò planeque invitò stultos et fatuos?

Socratem ferunt morti proximum de piorum immortalitate beatāque vitā quae mortem consequitur, disputavisse, itaque laeto ac libenti animo letale illud poculum hausisse—quasi non ad mortem, sed ad regnum atque imperium vocaretur.

[161] At verò, quorum animus in terrā defixus haeret, qui nihil nisi mortale terrenumque cogitant, eos plane repugnantes atque invitos e vitā discedere videmus. Nec immeritò, quum animorum aeternitatem propius iam intuentes crucientur mirum in modum, quasi flagitiose actam vitam poena etiam sit immortalis consecutura. Atque illud etiam—

that are obviously granted to no denizen of earth save man alone? Namely: to be an observer of the heavens and the goings on in the heavens, or to develop mastery of great and complicated subjects, whether they relate to improving morality, or gaining astronomical lore, or to training the mind and memory in advanced and complicated matters. [160] Don't such amazing privileges *prove* that the soul is divine, and that its nature is sampled and drawn from nowhere but the heavens?

### The Appeal to Attitudes toward Death

If souls did perish along with bodies, could the wisest among us *really* die so calmly? Would impulsive fools *really* resist death so frantically?

Moments before dying [*399 BCE*], we're told, Socrates was discussing the immortality of the righteous and the happy life that follows death. Hence he drained the poison cup willingly and cheerfully — as if he were being summoned not to death, but to inherit an empire.

[161] By contrast, when people's hearts remain fixated on earth, when they think only of crumbling, earthbound concerns, we see them dragged kicking and screaming out of life. And understandably so, since peering into the eternity of their souls is excruciating agony. They believe eternal punishment awaits their sinful lives.

("¡O stultum hominem," dixerit aliquis, "et naturae suae penitus ignarum!")

—nemini obscurum esse potest,

ex ipsis etiam sacris caerimoniisque maiorum aeternam hominis vitam facile cognosci atque intellegi posse. Neque enim illi aut mortuos tanto honore coluissent aut tam multas tamque varias sepulcrorum caerimonias posteris tradidissent, nisi cognitum perspectumque habuissent vigere animum in morte nec, quamquam corpus occidat, hominem ipsum penitus evanescere. [162] Itaque, statuisse videntur mortem ipsam non esse humanae vitae confectricem nec ex eā sequi interitum, sed potius ad aliam multo feliciorem vitam iis qui recte vixissent ducem optimam solere exsistere.

Quicumque enim convenienter naturae vixerint nec illam secuti sint malae consuetudinis corruptelam quae divinitus datos igniculos exstinguit vitiaque gignit et confirmat omnia, eos et viventes gloriā et e vitā excedentes praemiis prosequi oportet. Id enim non solum rationi consentaneum, sed etiam verissimum atque aequissimum est. ¿Cui autem aequitatis antiquior cura quàm deo?

It makes you want to scream: *Fool! How could you not know what birth meant?*

## The Appeal to Burial Customs

And yet the fact that human life is eternal can't be news to anyone; it can be easily known and understood from our ancestors' religious ceremonies and rituals. You see, they wouldn't have lavished such honor on their dead or left us all our various tomb ceremonies if they hadn't ascertained that the soul lives on in death, and that although the *body* passes into twilight, the *person* doesn't vanish completely. [162] They evidently wanted to instill in us that death is *not* the destroyer of human life, that it does *not* result in nonexistence. Rather, it serves, if we've lived morally, as our best guide to another and far happier life.

You see, when people live in accordance with nature, when they shun bad behaviors that suffocate our God-given potential and breed every vice, it's fitting for them to receive honors in life and tributes in death. That's not just reasonable, it's also the truest and *fairest* scenario. And who cares more about fairness than God?

[163] Itaque, quum homo—solus ex omni propemodum genere—nactus sit aliquam notitiam dei, nisi vitae iniquitate deo iniquus atque invisus evaserit, ad deum certe evolabit.

Idque aeternitatis humanae vel maximum ac firmissimum argumentum est, solum hominem divinae voluntatis participem consciumque exsistere ut, quamquam agrestibus silvestribusque in locis natus sit, tamen—ipsā docente naturā—et esse deum, et colendum ac verendum esse, dubitare non possit. [164] ¡O rem dignam in qua non modo homines, sed ipsas etiam pecudes obstipescere ac, si fieri possit, etiam erubescere oporteat:

- cognatum esse hominem deo;
- nullum aliud in terris animal—nisi hominem solum—dei cognitione imbutum esse;
- nec quidquam esse aliud quod animo e divinā mente hausto praeditum sit;

—tantamque inesse homini caecitatem atque socordiam ut, divinae cognationis immemor—¡¿aversetur migrationem ad deum?!

Nec enim aliud esse mors quàm migratio ad caelestes superasque sedes existimanda est—nec id solum ratione quadam aequitati veritatique consentanea, sed etiam sapientissimorum hominum maxime firmo stabilique consensu.

## The Appeal to Man's Sense of God

[163] Of virtually all creatures, man alone possesses some knowledge of God. Unless a life of evil makes him evil and hated by God, therefore, he'll surely fly to God.

And *that* is the single best and strongest argument for human immortality: that *man alone is cognizant of the divine will and has a role in it*. He can be born in the wild, in a jungle; doesn't matter. *Nature* inevitably teaches him that God exists and must be worshipped. [164] Isn't that *amazing*? It ought to awe men and beasts alike—shame them, too, if possible—that:

- Man is *related* to God.
- No animal on earth, save man alone, is imbued with *knowledge* of God.
- Nothing else in existence possesses *a soul drawn from* the Divine Intelligence.

Yet is man's blindness, his negligence, really so great that he *forgets* his divine relationship—and balks at *decamping* to God?!

You see, we must view death as nothing other than a decamping to the heavenly abode above. Reason proves the justice and truth of that view, and the long-standing, overwhelming consensus of our wisest thinkers confirms it.

Atqui eum qui hoc pacto vivere ac paene a se ipso dissentire velit, meminisse certe oportuit terram ipsam omniaque quae sub caelo sunt, divinā voluntate regi, proptereaque quiddam nobis quod observandum et addiscendum videatur praescribere. [165] ¿Quis ergo terram ipsam aut quotannis feracem aut semper optimas fruges et numquam malas inutilesque herbas ēdentem efferentemque vidit? ¿quis animalia semper uberes fetūs edidisse, numquam sterilitatem passa esse recordabitur?

Quod si haec ipsa secus se habent nihilque in rebus humanis perpetuò firmum eiusdemque naturae optare licet, ¿cur, quam in omnibus et rebus et animantibus vicissitudinem cernimus, eam ab homine seiungamus? Qui si multos annos feliciter vixerit, si sobolem, honores, opes adsequutus diu tantis bonis frui potuerit, praeclare secum esse actum vere dixerit.

[166] Sed adversi tamen aliquid subeundum perferendumque relinquetur: demum oppetenda mors erit—quae eo levior esse debet, quòd omnibus communis est nec cuiquam singularis aut praecipua; sed hoc quoque gratior, quòd nos a multis erroribus abstrahit quibus quoad vivimus, in tantā opinionum varietate adsiduāque veri inquisitione perturbari saepe solemus, et ad ipsam cernendam fruendamque veritatem iucunde traducit.

# HOW TO GRIEVE

## CHANGE AND DEATH ARE INEVITABLE—
## BUT LEAD TO HAPPINESS

Even those who choose to live in denial *must* have noticed that the earth and everything under heaven is regulated by the divine will, which, therefore, seemingly prescribes cues we ought to observe and learn. [165] I mean, please: who's seen the earth be fertile *every* year? *always* yield excellent crops? *never* weeds? Who can remember animals *always* producing viable offspring? *Never* sterile?

If that's not reality, if we can't hope for *anything* in life that's inherently fixed and unchanging, why exempt man from the same mutability we observe in every *other* creature and thing? If you've lived many years happily, if you've enjoyed years of children, honors, and wealth, then you can say it: you were dealt an amazing hand!

[166] That said, you'll still have *one* ordeal to suffer and endure: you must, in the end, face *death*. Death should be *manageable*, in that it's universal and not unprecedented or targeted at any one individual. It should also be *welcome*, in that all life long, we're surrounded by opinions and misguided notions that disorient us in our constant search for truth. Death plucks us out and gently guides us to recognize and enjoy truth itself.

Quo nihil beatius homini posse contingere satis ut arbitror, ex eo suspicari possumus, quòd innata est homini cupiditas scientiae; eius autem praestantia, non sane video qua aliā in re nisi in perfectā veritatis cognitione posita sit. Ex quo, fit ut veritatis cognitionem adsecuti perfectā absolutāque scientiā potiamur, vereque dici potest, qui veritatem intueatur sensuque percipiat, eum voti sui compotem vereque beatum esse.

[167] Quod si beata vita quaerenda nobis est nec quidquam fugiendum magis quàm ne miseriarum gravitate premamur, ¿quid illo homine stultius aut stolidius reperiri potest qui ceterorum morte ita angitur ut, beatae vitae oblitus, miseram atque infelicem consectetur?

Profectò enim ita se res habet ut nisi mortis dolorisque timore liberatus sit, etiam si multas cognitas perceptasque virtutes habeat rectumque et aequum omni plane utilitati anteponat, beatus tamen esse nemo possit:

- ¿Quid enim aliud dolor est nisi cruciatus animi isque perpetuus?
- ¿Quid aliud timor nisi adsiduus invisarum ac molestarum rerum metus?

*No happier fate can befall a man!* — That's a fair inference from the fact that the thirst for knowledge is *innate* in man; and where does knowledge *get* its beauty, if not from a total grasp of the truth? It follows, too, that once we've grasped the truth, we attain perfect and absolute knowledge — and in gazing upon truth, feeling it, *tasting* it, your dream comes true: you are perfectly happy.

## WE MUST GET FREE OF GRIEF IN ORDER TO BE HAPPY

[167] If the happy life is meant to be our goal and crushing misery our greatest aversion, what lunacy can be found to equal the man who gets so distraught at the death of others that he forgets that happy life and clings to this miserable, forlorn life?

The reality is, you *must* get free from fearing death and grief. Otherwise, even if you learn many virtues, internalize them, and sacrifice expediency to justice, there's simply no way to be happy. I mean,

- Isn't grief just another word for "merciless psychological torture"?
- Isn't fear just another word for "a nagging dread of real-life nightmares"?

[168] At ¿quomodo felix aut beatus esse poterit, qui assiduo cruciatu metuque urguebitur? Quin, eo miserior atque infelicior existimari debet quòd non solum sibi ipsi molestiam miseriamque comparabit, sed in ceterorum etiam sermonem ac vituperationem incurret. Nihil enim nimio dolore deformius, nihil a viro alienius.

Et, si corporis pravitatibus vituperatio proposita est, ¿vitiis ipsis quibus laborat animus, nihil turpitudinis, nihil inuretur infamiae?

Illa verò et graviora sunt et maiori animadversione vindicanda quo nobiliorem quàm corpus est sedem—nempe animum ipsum—occupaverunt.

[169] Quod si turpis dolor nimius et vituperatione dignus, certe illud consequetur, ut qui nimio dolori se ipsum tradat, ne laude quidem ullā dignus censeatur. Est enim series quaedam maxime veritati consentanea, ut sententiarum, sic rerum; et, quemadmodum in sermone disputationeque nostrā nectitur aliud ex alio, ita qui se unā aliquā vel deformitate vel turpitudine implicari patitur, multis statim miseriis ac deformitatibus opprimetur.

[170] Nec, verò, credi velim me, quia dolori nimio repugnem, idcirco dolorem omni ex parte improbare, omnesque illius ex animo fibras evellendas existimare. Est enim quatenus homo doleat, et—quod prudenter a Crantore dictum est—sive secetur pars aliqua corporis sive avellatur,

[168] Now, how can you be happy or content if you're plagued by torment and dread? You can't. You'll actually be *doubly* unhappy, because you'll not only be *creating* your own misery, you'll also attract gossip and criticism from others—because nothing is more unbecoming or unmanly than exaggerated grief.

Moreover, if abusing your *body* attracts criticism, do you expect that the vices the *soul* struggles with won't attract shame and stigma?

Actually, they're *more* compromising, *more* unacceptable, because the abode they've occupied—the soul—is nobler than the body.

[169] If exaggerated grief is disgraceful and merits rebuke, it follows automatically that if you give in to it, you're unworthy of *any* kind of praise. You see, things are linked like propositions in logic, and their chains lead to truth. In debates and discussions, each point is connected to the last. Similarly, if you let yourself get tangled up in one weakness or vice, you'll find yourself immediately overwhelmed and immiserated by many vices.

## ANGUISH IS OKAY WITHIN LIMITS

[170] But make no mistake. Just because I'm against *excessive* grief, doesn't mean I object to *all* pain or think its every last root must be torn from our souls. There's room for human anguish. As Crantor wisely remarked, if some part of our body gets amputated

183

sensus tamen adesse debet. Istuc enim nihil dolere fieri non potest quin, quemadmodum feritatem corporis quandam, sic animi stuporem maximum indicet.

[171] Sed nimirum illud est, quod improbamus, dolori nos ipsos ita tradere ut in aliam fortasse graviorem ex aliā parte vituperationem incidamus. Nam quemadmodum qui nihil prorsus doleat desciscere videatur ab hominis naturā—quae, morte perculsa, dolorem ac luctum aliquo modo indicare cogitur—ita, qui dolori nimis indulgeat, humanae naturae penitus oblivisci communemque omnium condicionem recusare iudicabitur. Quibus rebus intellegitur graviter peccare homines, quum vel ea quae omnibus perferenda subeundaque sunt, detrectare audent, vel quid ipsos in vitā deceat, quaeque sequi aut refugere debeant, non cernunt satis.

Quod proprium prudentiae munus est, quam humanarum actionum moderatricem a dis immortalibus esse constitutam infitiari nemo potest. [172] Atqui huic tam praeclaro divinoque muneri plane obsistit, qui nimio dolore ducitur. Non modo enim se ipsum sine ullo fructu lacrimis ac tristitiae tradit, sed etiam omni plane consilio ac iudicio vacat.

- ¿Ubi enim ratio, si se dolore auferri sinat?

or torn off, the feeling should still be there; you can't say "Doesn't bother me!" without implying a berserker mindset toward physical pain *and* the clarity of your brain.

[171] No, what I *do* object to is abandoning ourselves to grief so much that we find ourselves criticized for the opposite attitude, and maybe worse. You see, you'd come across as unnatural and inhuman if you felt *no* grief at all, since death is shocking and naturally forces out signs of pain and grief somehow. In the same way, if you *overindulge* in grief, people will say you're forgetting what it means to be human, that you're rejecting our universal condition. That shows how people go seriously astray when they dare refuse an ordeal we all must suffer, or when they can't weigh options and decide a best path forward for themselves.

Yet choice is the province of *discipline*, which the immortal gods undeniably set up as a brake on human behavior. [172] If you get carried away with excessive grief, it means you're completely rejecting this magnificent gift from the gods. And you aren't just surrendering yourself to tears and sorrow, which is pointless; you're also being completely illogical. I mean,

- Where's your reason, if you're letting yourself get carried away in grief?

- ¿Ubi constantia, si sibi ipse repugnet et in maerore iaceat?
- ¿Ubi denique humanitas, si se hominem esse oblitus nihil sibi cum morte commune esse contendat?

Iam verò illud stultissimum, existimare, quae ceteri homines libenti animo subeant, iis se non esse obstrictum. [173] ¿Quid enim? ¿an ignorare quisquam potest quanta inter homines cognatio sit quantaque similitudo? Etenim, nisi hoc verum fateremur, causae nihil esset cur homo hominem consilio, re, gratiā, iuvaret, ab hostium impetu ac laesione defenderet. Quod contra videmus accidere ut, qui ab his actionibus avertat animum, non modo in vulgus improbetur, sed etiam inhumanitatis ac feritatis accusetur.

Certe enim non e marmore sculpti aut e robore dolati sumus; est in nobis quiddam quod pietate misericordiāque moveatur nec exstingui sinat illam, qua dis proximi sumus, iuvandi ac bene faciendi voluntatem. [174] Itaque, insitum homini atque innatum videtur ut, quotiens alium hominem, quamvis alienum, premi calamitate atque aerumnā videat, crucietur animo nec, si facultas suppetat, dimittendam putet illius sublevandi occasionem. Quam

- Where's your character, if you're falling apart and crying on the floor?
- Where's your *humanity*, if you forget you're human and claim you have nothing in common with death?

But surely the dumbest thing is thinking you're not bound by the same restrictions that others submit to willingly. [173] I mean, please. Can anyone pretend the genetic similarities among people, our commonalities, aren't blindingly obvious? Because if we deny them, you couldn't explain why man aids his fellow man with advice, money, or influence, or defends him from the attacks of enemies. We see the opposite happen, though. Anyone who ignores such acts is not only unpopular, but even accused of selfishness and inhumanity.

## ON ALTRUISM AND CHARITY

You see, we aren't carved from marble or hewn from oak. There's something in us that's moved by pity and compassion, something that won't let us stifle the spiritual desire to help and support others. [174] It seems to be innate and instinctive in us that, every time we see another person down on their luck or in distress, even a total stranger, it tugs at our heartstrings. We feel that if it's in our power, we can't ignore an opportunity to help out. It's like

enim ipse, si eo loco esset, benignitatem sibi impartiri optaret, eā ut in alium utatur, natura tacitā quadam voce monere ac praecipere videtur.

Quae igitur sibi evenire posse dubitet, ea si contingant, ¿cur angi ac perturbari velit, aut ¿cur non potius humana illa esse et omnibus hominibus proclivia fateatur? [175] ¡Quanto rectius ille, qui

"hominem se *agnoscit*, nihilque humani a se alienum put*at*!"

Itaque, quum hanc ex animis nostris opinionem—mala omnia non esse humana—veluti immitem quandam et immanem beluam extraxerimus, profectò minus misere minusque sollicite vivemus. Relinquetur enim illa cogitatio, quaecumque accidant, fortiter ferenda esse nihilque posse homini evenire quo funditus prosternatur; idque ita erit, si nobismet ipsis non adsentabimur, sed veritatem, qua nihil praeclarius, praestabilius, uberius esse potest, toto pectore amplectemur. Haec enim illa est quam adsecuti, meliores multo efficimur et ad perferenda incommoda praeclaraque peragenda alacriores, [176] quum nihil, nisi quod rectum et aequum est, laudabile arbitramur, nihilque aliud nisi egregia illa ex quibus vera gloria nascitur, expetimus.

Nature's telling us in a silent "voice" to show the same kindness to another that we'd hope to receive if we were in that position ourselves.

So, if we doubt certain accidents can happen to us, but they do, why get distraught or upset? Why not admit instead that those accidents are part of the human condition and can happen to any of us? [175] Such was the wisdom of the sage who recognized:

"I'm human, and I think nothing human is alien to me."[24]

This idea that "evils aren't all part of the human condition" is like an invasive, predatory beast. Once we expunge it from our hearts, we will, rest assured, live life less anxiously, less miserably. It'll dawn on us that, come what may, we *must* endure it courageously, and that *nothing* can happen to man that should leave him lying in despair. And we'll get there if, instead of flattering ourselves, we wholeheartedly embrace the truth, which is the finest, most sublime, and most precious thing in the world. It's by facing the *truth* that we become better and more resilient in enduring adversity and accomplishing great tasks, [176] since we'll accept nothing other than what's fair and right, and we'll aspire to nothing less than the greatness that begets true glory.

Ac mihi videor nimis etiam nunc anguste atque exiliter agere. ¿Qui enim latior obiici campus queat in quo fidentius atque alacrius exsultare possit oratio?—Sed faciam impudenter, si medicinam deserens animorum, quam ex omnibus maxime utilem esse intellego, ad meam unius delectationem sermonem omnem mentemque convertam.

[177] Dolorem igitur nimis acrem ac diuturnum fugiendum diximus; et quidem probabiliter, quum ex eo mala multa maximeque gravia soleant exoriri, contra verò nihil boni.

Neque enim dolor ex illis rebus est, in quibus vel ad probandum vel ad vituperandum multa et magna contrariarum rationum paria momenta agnoscantur. Hoc enim si accideret, agerem verecundius neque me in eum locum demitterem, unde nullum plane exitum viderem. Sed, quoniam haec ita se habent, contendo vincendum esse animum dolorique acriter obsistendum. Sive enim nosmet ipsos sive vulgi opinionem cogitemus, id nobis sine ullā dubitatione faciendum est.

[178] At—si ad mortuos ipsos animum traducamus—¿quî possumus existimare gratum illis fore, quòd nimio dolore cruciemur? praesertim quum ex eo nihil ad illos utilitatis, sed permultum ad nos dedecoris atque incommodi permānet.

I feel like I'm still being too bare-bones, too reserved. Where can I find a *bigger* field for my rhetoric to prance and play with greater confidence and energy?—But, no: psychotherapy is the most helpful of all treatments, I know, and it'd be obnoxious for me to abandon it and divert my essay and concentration just to indulge myself.

## THE DEAD DO NOT WANT US TO GRIEVE

[177] I've said that searing, prolonged grief must be avoided; and rightfully so, since it tends to give rise to many very serious problems, and never anything good.

You see, grief isn't one of those things where you see many strong, equally valid reasons for and against it. If you did, I'd be less bold; I wouldn't let myself into a spot from which I see no way out. But that's the reality, so I reiterate my point that we must master our emotions and fight grief viciously. Whether it's our selves or our public persona we're thinking of, there's no question that *that* is what we must do.

[178] Moreover, consider the dead themselves. How could we imagine *they*'d enjoy us being wracked with grief, especially since it does *them* no good and it brings *us* enormous shame and distress?

¿Quid igitur eos ipsos a nobis optare atque expetere arbitremur? Nihil sane nisi ut eos illustri memoriā ac recordatione decoremus.

♫*Nemo me lacrumis decoret!*♫

ait Ennius. ¿Cur? Quia—

♫*volito vivus per ora virum!*♫

[179] ¿Quid, igitur, est causae cur fletum lacrimasque recuset? Nimirum, ea gloria quam se adhuc viventem adsecutum esse confidebat.

Eandem igitur ob causam, nostrum quoque luctum mortuis ingratum molestumque fore suspicemur, nec aliud eos a nobis quidquam flagitare credamus quàm ut id ipsum illis quo maxime delectamur, tribuamus. [180] Haec autem gloria est, et adsidua illorum virtutis recordatio; quam, si sermone laudationeque nostrā immortalem efficere liceat, hoc uno de mortuis nos vel optime meritos existimare possemus.


¿Quid, quòd eum qui sic doleat ut recreari confirmarique non possit, ne divinum quidem numen horrere, sapientissimi homines prodiderunt? [181] Impium autem est, quibus debemus omnia, iis pessimam referre gratiam;

So, what *should* we decide they want from us? Nothing at all, except for us to honor them with a few nice thoughts and remembrances. As Ennius says,

♫*No one should honor me with tears!*♫

Why? Because—

♫*I'm alive, everywhere, on the lips of men!*♫

[179] Why does he reject weeping and tears? Obviously, it's the glory he felt he'd won while still alive.

For the same reason, therefore, let's assume *our* grief will displease and annoy the dead. Let's believe they demand nothing more from us than that one tribute we love most, [180] namely glory, and forever remembering their good qualities. And if our words and eulogies were capable of making that glorious memory everlasting, then by that, and that alone, we could believe we've done our level best for the dead.

## WE MUST CULTIVATE GREATNESS AND GRATITUDE

What about the idea our greatest thinkers offer us, that if you let yourself sink irretrievably into despair, you're second-guessing God? [181] Well, it's sinful to repay those to whom we owe everything with rank ingratitude.

contra, verò, qui deorum voluntati paruerunt, nihilque se quod ab illis ultro daretur moleste ferre, declaraverunt, eos non solum viventes praecipuā laude ornavit antiquitas, sed etiam e vitā egressos perpetuo coluit honore, idque eo studiosius ac libentius, si quos intellexit cum deorum cultu exercitationem virtutis et praecipuam in mortales beneficentiam coniunxisse.

Scite profectò, ut cetera ferme omnia. [182] ¿Quid enim maiori laude dignum ex omnibus rebus humanis commemorare possimus quàm, eum qui vitam ducat cum virtute coniunctam, ad deorum cultum atque honorem perpetuum in homines studium ac pietatem adgregare? nec quidquam tantulum modo in eius animo exsistere quod non vel pietati vel humanitati vel denique virtuti sit consentaneum?

[183] Nec aliam sane ob causam perturbari omnem vitam errore inscitiāque videmus, nisi quòd, quae in hominis vitā praecipua esse deberent—pietas erga deos, in homines beneficentia, virtus in ingeniis ac moribus—ea fere omnia negliguntur, eādemque ratione, quae maxime vitare deberemus, ea studiose expetimus, caecoque impetu ferimur ad illa quibus vita nostra plane fera atque immanis efficitur. Ex hoc fonte cupiditates insatiabiles exoriuntur, quibus non modo singulos homines, sed totas familias et universas funditus eversas civitates videmus, praeterea seditiones, insidiae, discordiae rerumque et hominum clades et interitus. Ex his etiam incredibiles

By contrast, consider those who submitted to the gods' will and made clear they resented nothing the gods put in their path. Antiquity not only exalted them during their lifetimes, it also consecrated them with perpetual honors after they'd departed life—and did so all the more eagerly and enthusiastically for those who wedded *religious* devotion to personal greatness and generous philanthropy.

As so often, our ancestors were spot on. [182] I mean, what's more impressive in all the world than seeing a man of integrity crown an unwavering reverence for the gods with a total commitment to his fellow humans? And that in his heart, there isn't the slightest hint of anything at odds with piety, with humanity, or indeed, with greatness?

[183] And that explains exactly why we see all of life misaligned by ignorance and error. You see, the qualities that *ought* to be man's priorities in life—piety, philanthropy, and personal greatness—are practically all neglected. By the same token, we eagerly seek out the things we should most avoid; some blind striving impels us to embrace the things that utterly degrade and debase our lives. It's the source of insatiable desires which cause us to witness not only individual people, but whole families and entire civilizations wiped out. It gives rise to insurrections, plots, polarization, and the ruinous destruction of property and people. It also leads to

inconceivable heartache—heartache that inevitably makes life not just stressful and joyless, but horrific and bleak.

[184] It's a different world for those who cultivate greatness. By conforming to the will of the gods [*cf. 181*], they trust all that they have, not to themselves, but to the gods. They do no one harm; they embrace one and all with generosity, kindness, and love. They are beyond anxiety and beyond desire, because they've halted every onslaught of temptation and torn the roots of greed and craving from their souls.

## Great Souls Are Sainted in Heaven

It was natural, therefore, that when people had lived and died with a clear conscience, pleased the gods, and served their fellow man, our ancestors deemed them worthy of divine honors.

Our wisest poet [*Ennius*] had a point in declaring that they're spending eternity with the immortal gods.

Of course, he didn't say that because anyone could actually believe their *bodies* were taken up into heaven. There's no need to believe that, since Nature doesn't allow something that is *of* the earth to remain anywhere but *on* earth. No, he meant we believe their *souls* have been elevated to heaven,

[185] Quod de Romulo, urbis nostrae conditore, memoriae proditum accepimus; quem singulare in genus hominum collatum munus tam praeclarae urbis condendae in deorum numero collocavit—idque eo tempore quo litteris et doctrinis homines exculti facile fictum a germano, verum a falso secernebant, ut credi non possit quidquam illis persuaderi potuisse quod ullam ficti aut falsi imaginem prae se ferret.

[186] Sed, quòd ille mortalis eximiā virtutis ac beneficentiae gloriā consecutus est ut non solum immortalis, sed deus iudicaretur, id ipsum aliis etiam tributum esse ut inter deos recepti putarentur, quum excessissent e vitā, annales veterum loquuntur.

Quod et apud Graecos prius contigit et inde fortasse ad nostros permanavit. Nam et Hercules et Liber, fratres Tyndaridae, et feminae plurimae, quibus nunc inter deos locus esse praecipuus creditur, et hominibus nati et homines fuerunt. Sed, quòd virtute praestiterunt et ut ceteris ad recte vivendum beneque merendum praelucerent, elaboraverunt, ideo eos hominum fama, beneficiorum memor, in consessu concilioque caelestium collocavit.

because they belonged to people whose conduct toward the immortal gods and humankind merited the ultimate reward.

[185] Such, tradition tells us, was the fate of Romulus, founder of our city. His phenomenal contribution to humankind of founding this awesome city earned him admission to the ranks of the gods. What's more, that was already a time when people were enlightened by literature and science and could easily separate fact from fiction, truth from falsehood. They couldn't be hoodwinked into believing anything that smacked of falsehood or fabrication.

[186] But glory, greatness, and philanthropic service didn't just earn that mortal man belief in his *immortality*; they decided he was a *god*. Now, ancient chronicles tell us the same tribute was paid to others, too, so that upon dying, they were welcomed into the ranks of the gods.

This belief first arose among the Greeks and then apparently spread to us. For example, Hercules, Bacchus, Castor, Pollux, and a great many women who are now believed to occupy a special place among the gods, were no less human and no less born from humans.[25] But they made themselves great and endeavored to become a beacon to others in the ways of justice and humanity. Hence, in remembering their service, the awe of men found a place for them in the palace and pantheon of heaven.

Atque ipsos quos vocamus "maiorum gentium deos," aliosque quàm plurimos quos in deorum numerum rettulimus, hinc a nobis egressos et in caelum profectos facillimum erit agnoscere.

[187] Maximum verò argumentum est, quod de illis credimus, id esse verissimum, quòd et tantus tot saeculorum doctissimorumque hominum consensus veritatis vox ipsa esse videtur,

et quòd tantae tamque praeclarae virtuti quem alium vere congruentem locum tribuere oporteat, non sane reperies. [188] ¿Quis est autem tam demens ut, quos innocentiâ, liberalitate et singulari quadam ac praecipuā virtute dis proximos intellegat, iis seiunctum a dis tribuendum locum censeat?

Et, quum hominis animus terrena respuat, ad supera semper feratur; qui non solum tacito naturae impulsu, sed voluntate reque ipsā ut quàm maxime caelestibus similes essent, praestiterunt, eos ¿licebitne caelo esse privatos? [189] Mihi verò, eo iustius in caelo collocati videntur, quo clarior eorum inter homines vel eluxit liberalitas vel virtus enituit.

¿Quis enim Hercule fortior, ¿quis prudentior, ¿quis ab omni cupiditate remotior? ¿Quos ille <non> labores ut fortiter ageret et hominibus prodesset, suscepit et pertulit, aut ¿quid non doloris et calamitatis exhausit? [190]

It's also simple to see that even those we call "the original gods" started here among us before ascending into heaven. So did countless others that we've elevated to the ranks of the gods.[26]

[187] That said, the strongest validation of our belief about them is the overwhelming consensus of all those enlightened men over all those centuries. That consensus seems to be the voice of truth itself.

Besides, it's hard to imagine any *other* place suitable for true greatness such as theirs. [188] When you realize that their integrity, generosity, and unparalleled greatness puts them closest to the gods, you'd be out of your mind to think they deserve a place *separate* from the gods!

Moreover, given that our souls disdain earthiness and forever gravitate upward, can heaven *really* be denied to those who were so very heavenly, not only naturally and instinctively, but by their voluntary choices and actions? [189] My own view is that the brighter or better their generosity or greatness illuminated mankind, the more reasonable it is that they're in heaven.

Take Hercules, for example. Who was ever braver, more disciplined, or in better control of his appetites? What labors did he *not* take on and complete in order to flex his bravery and benefit mankind? What pain and reversals did he *not* suffer? [190] So, who could allow *heaven* being closed to

¿Quis, ergo, hunc caelo excludi patiatur, quum eius virtuti sempiterna gloria et laudis patuerit immortalitas?

Eademque ceterorum condicio est; quorum alius alio genere virtutis, omnes summis et singularibus vel in ipsos deos, vel in homines, meritis praestiterunt.

Itaque, tam egregiis eximiisque factis non infixas plumbo statuas, non arescentes triumphorum coronas satis diuturna persolvere posse praemia iudicatum est, sed florentiora stabilioraque munera quaesita sunt, quibus ornarentur ii qui virtutem, honestatem, gloriam otio, libidini, voluptati, vitae denique praetulissent.

Tamque id aequum est quàm illud decorum maximeque probandum, non easdem improbis sedes quas bonis atque integris post mortem esse propositas. [191] Intellexerunt enim ex maioribus nostris complures qui sapientiā praestiterunt, quum in dis aequitas praecipue vigeat eaque in eorum gubernatione appareat maxime, fieri non posse quin nequitiam sceleraque aversentur, quique ea in vitā exercuerunt, eos a se ipsis longissime seiungant.

Quod in vulgus ēdi verumque existimari, non modo rationi conveniens sed utile quoque inprimis est futurum. Nam si quid in hominum animis pietatis, si quid religionis inerit, certe ob hanc potissimum causam se a flagitiis

*him*, while the immortality of *renown* was open to his heroism?

And it's the same for others we look up to—each heroic in their own way, all of them superhuman in their devotion to gods or men.

People decided, therefore, that lead-wrought statues and fading crowns of laurel couldn't last long enough to reward such epic exploits. Instead, they sought more perennial and stable gifts to exalt those who chose greatness over comfort, honor over appetite, glory over pleasure, and indeed, over life itself.

## SIN LEADS TO HELL

If that's reasonable, moreover, it's no less appropriate for the good and morally upright to *not* have the same afterlife abode as the wicked. [191] You see, our wisest ancestors understood that justice thrives above all among the *gods*, and that it's most clearly visible in their works. Hence, they understood, the gods must necessarily abhor wickedness and criminality; they must keep those who pursued it in life as far away from themselves as possible.

Moreover, having that view spread among the masses and be regarded as true will prove not only reasonable, but enormously useful. You see, if there's any piety, any religious feeling in the souls of men, they will assuredly refrain from vice and

ac facinoribus abstinebunt, quòd impios ac nefarios homines a deorum concilio ac societate arceri iudicabunt.
[192] **Nec enim omnibus iidem illi sapientes arbitrati
sunt eundem cursum in caelum patēre. Nam vitiis et
sceleribus contaminatos deprimi in tenebras atque in
coeno iacēre docuerunt, castos autem animos, puros,
integros, incorruptos, bonis etiam studiis atque artibus
expolitos leni quodam ac facili lapsu ad deos, id est, ad
naturam sui similem pervolare.** [*V22*]

[193] Quod si ita est, certe nobis, quantum conniti animo
possumus, quantum diligentiā consequi, contendendum
atque elaborandum est ut ne ab iis segregemur quorum
est proprium vitā frui sempiternā ac beatā. Quod efficere, qui voluerit—omnes autem velle debebunt, qui se
ipsos diligere convenienterque naturae volent vivere—
numquam committet ut, quae ceteris exitiosa fore cred-
iderit, ea ipse persequatur. Neque enim in spem venire
poterit aut ignoraturos esse deos quae ipse agat, quum
divinam naturam nihil praeterire credibile sit, aut illa pro-
baturos, a quibus non modo di, sed etiam sani homines
abhorreant. ¿Quid enim turpius libidine, ¿quid taetrius
avaritiā, ¿quid detestabilius crudelitate? Quae, quamvis in

criminality—and for that exact reason, because they'll decide that impious and wicked people are cut off from communion with the gods. [192] **You see, those same sages didn't think the same route to heaven was available to all. They taught that those who pollute themselves with crime and sin are cast into darkness and languish in the mire, whereas chaste souls—pure, undefiled, unspoiled, perfected through good practices and pursuits— waft upward to the gods, gliding to join a nature like their own.**

## COURAGEOUS STRUGGLE LEADS TO HEAVEN

[193] If that's true, then we must absolutely strive with all our heart—must use every ounce of concentration—to ensure we don't get cut off from those who are privileged to enjoy eternal life and happiness. If that's what you want—and all who choose to love themselves and live in accordance with nature *ought* to want it—then you'll never elect to engage in activities you believe will lead others to damnation. You simply can't hope the gods are unaware of your conduct, since it's not credible that *anything* escapes divine omniscience, or that they'll approve of conduct that's not just repugnant to the gods, but even to normal people. Because what's more degrading than debauchery, more nauseating than greed, more horrific than

hominibus aliquando exsistant, tamen ab hominis naturā tam aliena sunt quàm humanum illud erit, si omnia nobis bona omniaque commoda expetamus.

[194] Atque in hoc comprimendae sunt cupiditates, quibus trahimur persaepe ad ea quae virtuti adversantur. Quod facillime perficiet, qui tam gloriosi facinoris exitum secum ipse adsidue cogitabit.

Tantaque est huius cogitationis suavitas ut, quod libenter alacriterque agimus, etiam sine labore peragamus. Idque in praestantibus laudisque appetentibus hominibus facile cernitur, quorum tanta esse solet vel in obeundis proeliis vel in agendis causis vel in contentionibus pro re publicā suscipiendis alacritas tantaque virtus ut, quod in iis rebus periculi aut laboris est, aut non sentiant aut pro nihilo ducant.

[195] Magnum enim est contendentis et ad gloriam anhelantis animi fomentum, magnum solacium spes futurae ac propinquae sive utilitatis sive gloriae: neque id solum in magnis, sed etiam in levioribus laboribus ac studiis. Quos enim cursus, quos venatio delectat, eos quamvis de viā fessos ac paene exanimes videas, numquam tamen minus alacres minusque concitatos animadvertas.

Iam honorum cupiditas ¿quid non in nostrā civitate laboris, ¿quid non sollicitudinis negotiique facessit?

cruelty? I know those vices are sometimes found in *humans*, but they're as alien to human *nature* as it is naturally human to desire every possible good and advantage for ourselves.

[194] In recognizing that, we must repress the cravings that too often attract us to things that impede greatness. Success will come most easily if we stay focused on the outcome of this glorious struggle.

Moreover, the focusing *itself* is so sweet that we'll do the job willingly and cheerfully, and we'll complete it with no trouble at all. You can actually see that in the case of exceptional and glory-seeking people. Their energy and commitment to facing military battles or fighting courtroom battles or to entering politics tends to be so great that either they don't feel the danger and exhaustions those undertakings entail, or they disregard them.

[195] You see, for a competitor locked in a struggle for glory, an incredible pain blocker or shock absorber is the hope of the immediate advantage or glory that awaits. That's true not only in major efforts and pursuits, but in minor ones, too. For example, you can see sprinters or game hunters exhausted and on the brink of collapse, yes, but never any sign that they're less committed or into it.

And elections! What headaches, what *nightmares* do our citizens *not* submit to in their ambitions to

[196] ¿Quotus tamen quisque est, qui se vel labore defatigatum vel prensationis molestiā curāque confectum audeat dicere?

Sic, quorum oculos virtutis splendor occupavit gloriaeque studium animos delenivit, ii nec laborem sentiunt; et, si tantus est ut aliquando erumpat, eo tamen non magno opere moventur. Toti enim in eo sunt ut prosint patriae immortalemque sibi nominis memoriam comparent.

Quam si quis negligendam ducat, omnemque hominis felicitatem recte factorum conscientiā metiri velit, is certe divinos honores, qui claris viris tribui consueverunt, numquam negliget. Etenim de dis ipsis, qui eosdem sibi honores asciverunt, pessime iudicasse videretur.

[197] Tanta autem eorum qui huius modi consuetudine delectati sunt, et sapientia et aequitas agnoscitur, ut dubitari non possit quin ipsi quod egerunt, a certā ratione proficiscatur. Quales numerare . . .

- . . . Lacedaemonas possumus, clarissimos et fortissimos viros, qui cives suos mortem pro patriā obeuntes divinis honoribus adficere solebant.

win? [196] And yet hardly one would dare say the effort exhausts him, or that the campaigning leaves him wracked with anxiety.

*That* is the model. When the splendor of greatness fills your eyes and the pursuit of glory captivates your heart, you don't feel fatigue. Even if you do finally become aware of it, it hardly makes any difference, since you're so completely in the zone to help your country and immortalize your name.

And even if you think that's negligible—that the satisfaction of a job well done is good enough—you obviously can't discount the divine honors traditionally granted to heroic men. Otherwise, you'd seem to be disparaging the very gods who accepted those same honors themselves.

## APOTHEOSIS AND THE FOSTERING OF GREATNESS

[197] As for the peoples who *introduced* that practice [*of declaring men gods*], their wisdom and impartiality are so celebrated that they undoubtedly had some *reason* for doing what they did. Among them we can count:

- The Spartans. Those courageous and illustrious heroes would traditionally bestow divine honors on citizens who fell fighting for their homeland.

- ¿Quid verò illae, omnis plane doctrinae omnisque sapientiae parentes, Athenae? ¿nonne Codrum, regem suum, ob pietatem in patriam meritaque illa quibus excelluit, magno consensu in deos rettulerunt?

[198] Atque haud scio an recte senserint viri doctissimi, quorum ea fuit opinio, viros claros et fortes idcirco deorum immortalium honore consecratos ut incitaretur virtus acrius, et acuerentur vehementius ad obeunda pericula, qui patriae amore studioque tenebantur. Vera enim virtutis merces gloria est, nec quidquam est aliud quo magis ad recte honesteque agendum praestantis animi homines incendantur. Quod optime agnovit ac diutissime retinuit omnium litterarum praeclara custos et altrix Graecia, quae multos habet virtutis gratiā factos ex hominibus deos, quorum alios fatentur novos, alios multis iam saeculis receptos in caelum consecratosque contendunt; quàm multi autem sint, qui reconditas eorum scrutantur litteras, nosse fortasse possunt.

[199] Neque, verò, haec a me ideo copiosius disputantur quòd eos temere, neque satis considerate, tam multos consecratos esse credi velim, quum eos ipse quoque venerer deorumque loco habendos putem;

sed potius, quum tot apud omnes paene gentes immortalitate divinisque honoribus adfecti reperiantur, ut

- And what about that famed cradle of education and wisdom, Athens? In recognition of his exceptional patriotism and services, didn't they enthusiastically vote to deify their King Codrus [*eleventh century BCE*]?

[198] I do tend to think some highly enlightened minds were right to decide that the deification of great heroes was contrived to foster courage and a gung-ho attitude in patriots. You see, *glory* is the true reward for courage, and nothing can inspire a high-minded person to virtuous action more. The best country to realize that, and the one to practice deification longest, was Greece. That illustrious patron of arts and sciences has made *many* gods out of people in recognition of their greatness. Some of them, they grant, are recent, while they maintain others were canonized and received into heaven many centuries ago. If you scrutinize their arcane literature, you might be able to find out the total number.

[199] That said, I haven't been speaking about these issues at such length because I want to suggest they were all deified impulsively or unthinkingly. Indeed, I revere them myself and do think they should be considered gods.

No, I'm struck that we find that so *many* have been paid the tribute of immortality and divine honors, and among practically all nations. My aim,

exacuam bonorum mentes ad ea promerenda quae sapientium iudicio ducuntur amplissima.

Nihil enim praestantius aut beatius accidere homini
potest quàm eo loco donari in quem, ut ascenderent urbis
nostrae conditores, nullum periculum, nullum laborem,
nullum denique certamen praetermiserunt.

Ac, si privatae utilitatis et commodi habenda ratio est,
nullam aliam expetere aut optare vir sapiens et eruditus
praeter hanc unam debet.

[200] Templa, verò, publice vota et dedicata ¡quantum
in vulgus dignitatis, ¡quantum habent gloriae! quum
omnes qui deos illos quibus templa voventur, publice col-
unt, fateri cogantur et fuisse homines et ad deos divi-
nosque honores unā virtute fretos ascendisse.

[201] Nec mirandum est deos illos publice coli eorum-
que delubra et templa auguste sancteque exornari, qui
vel patribus nati sunt dis vel matribus. Nam quemadmodum eorum cultus et sanctus et religiosus est maximeque pietati atque aequitati consentaneus, sic admira-
tionis aut dubitationis nihil habet. Totus enim ex naturā
oritur ut iure ipso naturae, qui deo satus vel deā editus
procreatusque sit, deus esse debeat;

therefore, was to inspire the minds of good people to earn the rewards that our sages deem greatest.

You see, man can meet with no finer or more blessed fate than admission to a place that our founding fathers avoided no danger, no struggle, and no suffering to ascend to.

And if it's just one's own best interests we take into account, then *this* is the one and only reward which an enlightened and educated man should desire or aspire to.

[200] And just *look* at the awe and pride that's inspired in the masses by the temples that are vowed and dedicated to them! And naturally so, since anyone who worships those temple gods in public has to admit those gods were once people, and that by greatness alone they ascended to the ranks of the gods and acceded to divine honors.

[201] It's also no surprise that gods born of god fathers or god mothers are publicly worshipped, and their shrines and temples kept reverentially and piously adorned. Worshipping *them* is holy, religious, and fully consistent with piety and propriety, so it's not surprising or concerning at all; it's natural, a simple matter of birth. The very laws of pedigree dictate that a child born of a god or goddess ought to be a god.

at verò, qui homine patre vel mortali matre natus est, hunc esse deum et magnum quiddam videri potest et dubitandi occasionem nec fortasse ineptam multis adferre solet. [202] Non enim, si eximius talium virorum virtuti tribuatur honos, quin id iure fiat, aut dubitare aut negare quisquam potest; sed, quòd tantam virtutis esse vim velimus ut vel natura ipsa eius unius ope immutetur, hoc illud est de quo quaerere doctiores viri non immeritò soleant.

Quibus ita responsum est, non immutari virtute naturam; nec enim id sine prioris naturae corruptione posse evenire, sed eādem in illis manente naturā evolare animum ad deos et in eorum ascribi concilium, quum immortalis sit et immortalitatis divinae particeps; corpus autem suapte naturā mortale manere in terrā, quodque terrenum est, nullo pacto suam exuere posse naturam ut alienam induat.

[203] Quamvis enim haec ipsa quaestio perobscura videri soleat nec omnino proclives aut faciles habeat explicatūs, tamen, nisi auctoritatibus contra rationem pugnetur, non incommode, opinor, a nobis exposita censeri potest.

By contrast, it can sound counterintuitive for a person born of a *human* father or *mortal* mother to be a god. For many, that tends to give rise to not-entirely-unwarranted skepticism. [202] It's not that anyone doubts or denies that if the greatness of such heroes is granted extraordinary honors, then they're *granted* legitimately. No, it's our idea that greatness *itself* has some power to actually transform biology. *That* is the point where educated people tend, not unreasonably, to become quizzical.

In reply, however, they've been told that greatness does *not* transform biology, that that'd be impossible without fundamentally changing the person, and that their genetic makeup remains intact when the soul flies to the gods and is initiated into their company, since the soul is immortal and a partner in divine immortality, while the body, which is mortal by nature, remains on earth, and there's no way that something of the earth can shed its nature and don one that's alien to it.

[203] I realize this question seems very obscure and doesn't have any ready or easy answers. Still, unless I've contradicted the authorities unreasonably, I do believe I've discussed it somewhat successfully.

Et quoniam quae in hoc genere praecipua cognituque digna sunt, persequimur omnia—volumus quidem certe—, praetereundum non est quales, quàmque multae, virtutes erudiendorum hominum gratiā sint honore deorum immortalium consecratae. Cuius rei finis est publica utilitas ut, quo honore virtutes ipsas decoratas videant, eundem se consecuturos esse homines sperent, si iisdem virtutibus excellant.

[204] Quo in genere, multum boni est in imitatione. Libenter enim ea imitantur et persequuntur multi, ex quibus alios illa eadem quae ipsi appetunt, consecutos vident. Atque ex eo plerùmque accidit multis in rebus quas antea ne cogitaverant quidem, quum ad clarorum virorum imitationem se contulerint, multorum vigeat industria. Quae quum paulo manavit latius, quantos progressūs quantaque acquirat incrementa, nihil necesse arbitror commemorare.

[205] Constat enim inter omnes, quae praeclara ducuntur, ea fere omnia a tenuibus initiis sumpsisse exordium. Quod paulatim imitatione progrediente confirmatum ita increbruit ut ne augeri quidem aut exaggerari magis posset.

Quod si ullā in re gratum nobis atque optatum esse debet, certe in complectendis provehendisque virtutibus

## HEROIC AND SAINTLY MODELS ARE INSPIRING

And since I'm chasing down everything important or worth knowing on this topic (or trying to, anyway), I must also address the number and different *forms* of greatness that have been canonized in a bid to inspire and uplift humankind. The goal of those efforts is public improvement, to impress on people that they too can hope to attain those honors if they achieve the same kind of greatness.

[204] On that topic, a great deal of good lies in imitation. A lot of people willingly seek out and imitate the actions they see as responsible for others getting the things they want themselves. Hence, it frequently happens that modeling themselves on great men awakens a sense of heroism for many, and in many situations they'd never even thought about before; and once heroism starts pumping, needless to say, it makes rapid gains in progress and musculature.

[205] You see, it's common knowledge that virtually all great things start from small beginnings. Step-by-step imitation is what gradually bolsters and develops them to a point where they cannot rise or increase further.

Hence, if there's any area where we should endorse imitation, I can't see any more worthy for

non video quid esse possit optatius. Siquidem ex his
informatio pendet educatioque vitae, quae quum recte
instituitur atque excolitur, incredibile dictu est quantos
quàmque uberes iustitiae, integritatis omnisque amplis-
simae laudis fructūs adferat.

[206] Sed, quum virtutes multae meritò colantur, quòd
et ipsae cultu dignae sint et multae ab iis ad universum
genus hominum utilitates proveniant, quid sit cur bestiae
quoque ipsae ab Aegyptiis ferme omnes consecratae sint,
scire sane velim.

Sit piscis in cultu ac deorum opinione apud Syros, homines nec tantā ingenii acie praeditos nec tantis doctri-
narum praesidiis instructos ut haec inepta ridiculaque
esse possint agnoscere.

[207] Aegyptii verò—omnibus adfluentes eruditionis
et scientiae laudibus—quomodo in tam inanem tamque
absurdam delabi opinionem potuerint, equidem intellegere vix possum. ¿Quid enim? ¿an boves, canes, lupos,
feles, pisces in deorum numero habebimus, et quas nobis natura praesidii auxiliique causā animantes genuit,
eas per inscitiam deos iudicabimus? quibus nihil foedius,
obscaenius, lutulentius ne natura quidem ipsa viderit.

218

embracing and developing a sense of greatness. It's what the choices that shape our lives depend on, and when it's properly inculcated and fostered, the benefits and accumulative advantages that it bears—justice, integrity, and glory—are beyond description.

## MAN HAS SEEN FIT TO DEIFY LESS WORTHY CANDIDATES

[206] *Many* forms of greatness are deservedly revered, not only because they are inherently worth cultivating or worshipping, but also because they produce many boons for the whole human race.[27] Hence, I really would like to know why the Egyptians have deified *animals* as well—and practically all of them.

I have no problem with a fish being regarded and worshipped as a god [*Atargatis*] among the Syrians, people who aren't bright or educated enough to realize how stupid and ridiculous that is.

[207] The *Egyptians*, though?—so widely hailed for their enlightened learning? I just can't understand how *they* could wind up with such a pointless and absurd belief. I mean, shall we include cows, dogs, wolves, cats, and fish among the gods? Shall ignorance lead us to see gods in the animals Nature bore to protect and serve us?! Pfft! Not even Nature *herself* has seen anything as filthy, disgusting, or unclean as they are. [208] Will we also

[208] ¿Etiamne animalium monstra illa, a quibus hominum generi praecipua incommoda inferuntur—crocodilos,
aspidas, serpentes, ceteras feras et immanes beluas—in
deorum numerum referemus? ¿Quid erit aliud <quam>
naturam invertere et ima summis, summa infimis commu-
tare? Et, quum tantam in his imperitiam barbariamque ag-
noscamus, ¿tamenne ista penitus inania pertinaciter de-
fendemus? Eādemque inscitiā caepas, allia, fructūs ceteros
qui oriuntur e terrā, in deorum numero reposuit Aegyptus.
[209] Quae haud scio cur longiori oratione refellere sit
necesse. Incredibilis est enim eorum absurditas, ut nulla
esse possit aut pertinacia aut imperitia tanta quae non ista
aspernetur atque refugiat.

Imbres autem, nimbi, procellae si a nostris consecratae sunt, id antiquissimis populi Romani ritibus ac caeri-
moniis receptum et confirmatum est. Quae tolli aut perturbari, quum et satis firmā ratione nitantur et usu iam
ipso confirmata et approbata sint, sine nefario scelere non
possunt.

[210] Graeciam, verò, quam paulo ante laudibus or-
navimus, hoc loco non sane laudare possumus, quae Cu-
pidines et Amores satis audacter et temere in gymnasiis
aedibusque publicis consecrarit. ¿Quid enim Cupidini aut

include those monstrous animals that inflict enormous damage on humankind—crocodiles, asps,
snakes, all the other wild and bloodthirsty beasts:
we'll make *them* gods, too!? That'd mean no less
than flipping the natural hierarchy on its head—and
even though we recognize the utopian voodoo
behind *that* idea, will we stubbornly defend *these*
thoroughly bizarre ideas [*deifying animals*] all the
same?—And by the same magical thinking, Egypt
has set onions, garlic, and all the other vegetables
that grow out of the ground among the ranks of the
gods. [209] I don't know that it's necessary to re-
fute these ideas at great length; their absurdity is so
palpable that even the greatest stubbornness and ignorance in the world wouldn't try to defend them.

That said, if our own countrymen *did* deify rain-
storms, thunderclouds, and whirlwinds, well,
those deifications were *welcomed* and *confirmed* by
the most ancient rites and ceremonies of the Roman
people. Abolishing or tampering with them—
inasmuch as they're grounded in relatively solid
reasoning, and they're confirmed and validated by
experience itself—is impossible without unleashing
major disruption.

[210] As for Greece, which I was just heaping
praise on [*197–198*], well, I really can't praise it on
this score, since it *did* consecrate statues of Cupid
and the Erotes in gyms and public buildings. That

Amoribus cum gymnasiis? aut ¿quid ea consecratio vel ad considerandum vel ad imitandum adferre potuit honestatis aut boni?

[211] Nihil enim temerarium, nihil insipiens in deorum consecratione esse debet nec quod ullam vel levissimam aut turpitudinis aut ullius omnino impudentiae suspicionem adferat. Quales videri possunt eorum consecrationes, quorum in rebus probitati pudorique contrariis numen esse potentiaque creditur.

Qui, ergo, ad hominum vitam vel adiuvandam vel excolendam atque exornandam aliquid attulerunt, quique virtutibus rerumque gestarum gloriā praestiterunt, eos nemo dubitet iure deos habitos divinoque cultu adfectos esse.

Neque ego ullo pacto auderem hoc primus prodere. Non enim tam studiose quae laudari possunt appeto, quàm reformidare ea soleo, ex quibus possit aliquid vel levioris culpae redundare. [212] **Quum, verò, et mares et feminas complures in deorum numero esse videamus et eorum in urbibus atque agris augustissima templa veneremur, adsentiamur eorum sapientiae quorum ingeniis et inventis omnem vitam legibus et institutis excultam constitutamque habemus.** [*V23*] Tantis enim

took some nerve and might not have been the wisest idea, because what do allegories of sexual desire have to do with a *gym*? What lessons in honorable conduct or greatness could *those* deifications inspire for reflection or imitation?

[211] In consecrating gods, there's no place for anything impulsive, unwise, or that could cast even a *shadow* of suspicion, either of disgrace or of any misconduct whatsoever. Such can be the implication, however, of deifying gods whose power and will are thought to lie in things that go against chastity and morality.

## LEGITIMATE APOTHEOSES

Let no one doubt, therefore, the legitimacy of hailing as gods, and inscribing in the pantheon, those who contributed to helping or improving and elevating human life, and whose greatness and magnificent accomplishments brought them glory.

I'd never dare propose *inventing* this practice, since I'm not as interested in praise as I am afraid of getting even indirectly implicated in a scandal. [212] **But since we see among the gods quite a few men and women whose august temples we venerate in cities and countrysides, let's acknowledge the wisdom of those whose creative genius gave us laws and institutions to regulate and improve our lives.** With such guides we cannot go astray,

ducibus, aberrare non possumus, nec a nobis, sed ab illis ipsis quos sequimur, rei tam iustae ac debitae ratio reposcetur. Iure enim fecisse putandi sunt, qui, ne quem virum aut feminam praeclare meritam debito honore spoliarent, eorum memoriam sanctam venerandamque esse voluerunt.

Nos autem iniuste ageremus, si, quos pari cultu venerationeque dignos cognovimus, eos pateremur silentio praeteriri.

[213] Neque hoc de te unā, mea Tullia, dictum volumus, cuius exstabunt virtutis, prudentiae, doctrinae, continentiae ad omnem aeternitatem impressa vestigia, sed de iis omnibus quos tali honore dignos aut ipsi vidimus aut futuro tempore posteritas intuebitur.

Nunc autem de te loquar, quam non ego amissam aut mihi penitus ademptam velim dicere, quum illucescat menti meae cotidie magis praeclarissima nominis tui tuarumque virtutum gloria. [214] Vigebis autem memoriā, quamdiu monumenta exstabunt illa quibus eximia consignata sunt tam excelsae laudis testimonia; quae sempiterna fore, quum praestantissima sint, plane confidere debemus.

and an accounting of such an appropriate practice will be demanded, not of us, but of those we follow. You see, those who sought to prevent any man or woman from being denied the proper reward their merits deserved must be thought to have acted *legitimately* in wanting to make their memory sainted and venerable.

And *we—I*—would be acting *unjustly* if we allowed candidates we *know* to be worthy of the same worship and adoration, to get passed over in silence.

## THE APOTHEOSIS OF TULLIA

[213] And with these words I don't mean just you alone, my darling Tullia, though your greatness, wisdom, knowledge, and temperance have left traces for all eternity. I have in mind *all* of those we've witnessed ourselves, and that posterity will someday recognize as worthy of such honors.

Now, though, I *will* speak of you—though I refuse to call you "lost" or "utterly taken from me," since the glory of your name and your greatness dawns and enlightens my thoughts every day. [214] You'll live alive in memory, as long as monuments bearing brilliant witness to your towering glory shall stand—which, *because* they're so beautiful, I must hope will last for all time.

Tibi, igitur, numquam me debitum persolvisse officium putabo, nisi <te> de me optime meritam quem eximie coluisti ac de patriā quam semper ornasti, supremo honore decoravero. Id autem facile consequar, quum is locus quem tibi delegi, sempiternam habiturus sit religionem.

[215] Nostra, verò, si qua erit ex eā re consolatio, quae magna certe erit, aut si qua laus ex paternā pietate, mihi certe iucundissima acciderit.

Nihil enim aliud vel audire vel memoriā repetere libentius possum quàm

*me in eam quam summe dilexerim, summeque*
*diligendam merito suo censuerim, quàm maxime*
*pium gratumque esse*

—quum praesertim in alienos, quia de se optime erant meriti, tam prolixos liberalesque sese et maiores nostri et exteri praebuerint.

[216] **Quod**

- **si ullum umquam animal consecrandum fuit,**
  qualia multa consecraverunt Aegyptii, quod nullum **profectò fuit;**
- **si Cadmi aut Amphitryonis progenies aut Tyndari in caelum tollenda famā fuit;**

And that means I'll never consider my duty to you complete if I fail to glorify you—you who loved me dearly, who deserve the best from me and from the country that you graced—with the *ultimate* honor. And I'll succeed, I will, since the place I've chosen for you[*r shrine*] will be venerated for eternity.

[215] If my efforts console anyone, though, as they surely will, it'll be me. If a father's devotion can add some glory, *I*'ll be the one to revel in it.

There's no thought, you see, that I can hear said, or replay in my mind, more wonderful than this, that

*For the daughter that I loved absolutely, and who deserved and won my absolute love, I am eternally devoted and thankful.*

—especially since the ancients, both our own and those of other nations, lavished similar honors even on strangers who'd done their best by them.

[216] **On that point,**

- **If ever a creature was found worthy of deification that was actually utterly *unworthy*,** such as many the Egyptians deified, **and**
- **If fame merited the children of Cadmus, Amphitryon, and Tyndarus elevation to heaven,**[28]

huic īdem honos certe dicandus est.

Quod quidem faciam, teque omnium optimam doctissimamque approbantibus dis immortalibus ipsis in eorum coetu locatam ad opinionem omnium mortalium consecrabo. [*V23*] Tu, ergo, in eo ipso fano quod ad nominis tui memoriam ac cultum votum dedicatumque est, et laudari te et coli senties.

Maxime, autem, laetaberis in eo, quòd et eum tibi quem maxime debui honorem persolverim, et me simul iniquissimo fortunae imperio penitus exsolverim. Nosti enim quàm semper alacri fortique animo cunctis casibus restiterim, ut ne me quidem pulsum patriā omnique plane dignitate spoliatum tam acri impetu frangere ac deiicere fortuna potuerit. [217] Cum inimicis autem quantā contentione decertaverim, quaeque mea fuerit in iis refutandis frangendisque virtus et constantia, norunt omnes qui varios civitatis nostrae casūs curiose notaverunt.

Quum verò, Tullia, te mihi extremo loco fortuna ademisset, tum equidem intellexi quantum illa in rebus posset humanis quantāque adversùs me ipsum vi ac potestate niteretur. Itaque, nihil habui quod dicerem, nisi **cedo et manum tollo** [*V3*], quum tam gravi accepto vulnere, plane dolore perculsus atque adflictus essem.

then surely *she* deserves to be paid the same honor!

And I'll do that, Tullia, my wonderful, enlightened daughter. With the approval of the immortal gods themselves, I'll place you in their company. I'll raise you up as a god in the imagination of all mortals. You'll feel yourself being worshipped and praised in the shrine I've vowed and dedicated to the memory of your name and your glory.

Most of all, though, you'll be glad that I've paid *you* the honor I owed you most, and at the same time, redeemed *myself* from the ruthless demands of Fortune. You see, *you* know the resilience and fortitude with which I always resisted every setback. Fortune and her bitter onslaught failed to stop or break me, even far from home in exile, when I'd been stripped of all my dignity. [217] The determination I fought my enemies with, and the courage and calm I displayed in thwarting and crushing them—they're known to *everyone* who watched the shifting troubles of our country.

But when Fortune took *you* from me, Tullia, it was the final straw. It was only then that I truly *understood* her power over human affairs, understood the true extent of the violence she'd mustered against me. And the only thing left I could say was this: *I give up. It's over.* I was so badly wounded, grief completely overwhelmed and defeated me.[29]

## TULLIA IN HEAVEN AND THE TRIUMPH OVER DEATH

But now the lessons of wisdom have hardened me against all the violence of Fortune, and *you* are a god in heaven. It fills me with all the pleasure and happiness a heart can hold. I'm trembling all over with joy, and I triumph in victory over Fortune and all her sorrow.

Tullia, the awesome glory and memory of your greatness and your virtues were always of such wonderful help to me. Now that you're apart from mortals, don't forsake me! No, turn your eyes toward me. *Lead* me to the place where, at long last, I can look upon and speak with you. That way, *you* can repay the father who loves you with all his heart, repay him however you like; and *I'*ll make sure that the joy of our reunion eclipses all the heartache and pain I felt at saying goodbye.

## THE END

# NOTES

1. Robert Harris's 2015 novel *Dictator* brings these sad events vividly to life. Long before him, in the third century CE, the Roman historian Cassius Dio composed an imaginary scene of Cicero being consoled on his exile by a man in Macedonia (*Roman History* 38.18–29).

2. *Divine Institutes* 3.28. This passage is reflected in sections 216–217 of our treatise.

3. *Tusculan Disputations* 4.63, *naturae vim attulimus* (reflected in sections 5 and 87 here), and *Letter to Atticus* 12.14.3 (March 8, 45 BCE): *Quin etiam feci, quod profecto ante me nemo, ut ipse me per litteras consolarer.*

4. Voltaire 1765 in Appelgate 1974, 45; his adjacent essay, "An Important Study by Lord Bolingbroke" (ibid., 93–214) discusses the evolution of Christianity. Cicero himself believed in heaven, but not in hell (*Tusculan Disputations* 1.10 and elsewhere; the statement in section 192 here is an aberration); two centuries later, in his own treatise *Grief*, Lucian— the Voltaire of his times—laughs at the very idea of hell. King 2020 examines traditional (pagan) Roman attitudes toward death and the afterlife.

5. Graver 2002 collects the fingerprints of Crantor in the *Tusculan Disputations*; Curtius 2021 is the finest translation.

6. Forsyth et al. 1999.

7. The text was originally printed in book 4 of his letters, and then reprinted in his translation of *The Complete Works of St. Plato*. The quote appears in the subsection titled "Quantum Plato Neglexit..."

8. In his third and final defense, printed posthumously, Sigonius affirmatively denied it (Garisendus 1599, 11–12): "I neither wrote nor published this book, nor advised anyone else to publish it. All I did was believe in it once it was published..." It may be significant that Sigonius doesn't deny knowing who wrote it. I agree with McCuaig 1989 that Sigonius's various defenses of the text seem to demonstrate bad faith.

9. Baltussen 2013.

10. Theophrastus (371–287 BCE) was head of Aristotle's Lyceum. His lost book *Callisthenes: On Grief* espoused the maxim "Fortune, not wisdom, rules life" (quoted by Cicero as ♩*Vitam regit fortuna, non sapientia*♩ in *Tusculan Disputations* 5.25). Xenocrates (396–314 BCE) was head of Plato's Academy and Crantor's teacher. No book on grief by him is attested elsewhere, but he did write a treatise *On Death*. In the Renaissance, Marsilio Ficino claimed the pseudo-Platonic *Axiochus* was that treatise. Since *Axiochus* is a consolation, it seems likely that our author followed Ficino's lead (see note 7 above)—and

hence committed a blunder that hints at the Renaissance origin of our text.

11. An astonishing statement, and all the more amazing because "the one word" that sums up woman's misery, *parére* (obey), looks the same as *párere* (to bear children).

12. The Syrian poet Archias, whom Cicero defended on a charge of illegal immigration 17 years before his daughter's death, has an epigram on this very theme (*Greek Anthology* 9.111 = Gow-Page 18):

Praised be the Thracians! because—get this—they
     *grieve* for their children
   coming here into the light out of their mothers'
     womb.
By contrast, they *bless* everyone who departs this
     existence
   when Fate's apparitor, Doom, snatches them each
     by surprise.
Why? Because, whereas the living endure the gamut
     of heartaches
   all life long, the dead finally discover their cure.

13. In Latin more obviously than English, "nature" means "birth."

14. The tale of Silenus (which features in Nietzsche's *Birth of Tragedy*), the séance, and the fragment of Euripides alluded to (a famous passage of the lost *Cresphontes*, fr. 449) all appear in *Tusculan Disputations* 1.114–115. The first two are also found in Plutarch's

*Consolation to Apollonius* (27, 14), along with other quotations from Euripides' *Cresphontes* (15). The common source is obviously Crantor's treatise *Grief*.

15. As explained in the introduction, this quotation comes not from Plato but Marsilio Ficino's Renaissance-era *Life of Plato*.

16. Fabricated to look like a snatch of Homer or Ennius.

17. A word to the wise, since we still hear this line of argument on occasion: In *Tusculan Disputations* 1.83, Cicero states that Ptolemy II Philadelphus (308–246 BC) banned the teaching of this irresponsible idea in schools because students began taking it seriously, and committing suicide. (In particular, he censored one teacher, Hegesias of Cyrene, who'd written a book on the topic titled *Fatal Fortitude*.)

18. Plausible, but fabricated. Gorgias died at the age of 107.

19. Cicero is making an untranslatable connection here between fortitude and *fortis vir*, the usual Latin expression for a "real man."

20. This glorious quotation is a total fabrication. The implication of "somewhere" is "not in *Callisthenes: On Grief*" (see note 10).

21. A famous scene too laconically told here. *Tusculan Disputations* 1 and Xenophon *Hellenica* 2.3.56 have the fuller version.

22. This was to be Cicero's own fate in 43 BCE.

23. Ennius's *Epicharmus* fragments 7 and 8.

24. Terence's *Self-Tormentor* 77, a famous quotation that was to have a rich heritage.

25. One example of a deified woman is Ino, daughter of Cadmus. She became the goddess Matuta.

26. In *City of God* 8.5, Augustine claims these "original gods" include Jupiter, Juno, and others. He adds that one scholar sought to interpret them allegorically, as elements of the universe, but that they were really originally human.

27. A fascinating exploitation of the two meanings of *colere*: (1) to cultivate and (2) to worship. The author transitions from speaking about the private cultivation of greatness (*virtus*) in one's personal development, to the Roman public practice of worshipping the abstract Virtues as goddesses, complete with priests and temples: a cult.

28. Their children are respectively Ino, Hercules, and the brothers Castor and Pollux.

29. Allegedly, Cicero's exclamation is the cry of a defeated gladiator "tapping out."

# BIBLIOGRAPHY

*For a full list of source quotations used by the forger, see* http://classicsprof.com/ciceros-consolatio/. *Cicero gives his own views on grief counseling in* Tusculan Disputations *3.76–79 (Curtius 2021, 178–180). Ignatieff 2021 is virtually a companion piece to* How to Grieve, *and is warmly recommended.*

Appelgate, Kenneth W. (trans.). 1974. *Voltaire on Religion: Selected Writings.* New York: Frederick Ungar.

Baltussen, Han. 2013. "Cicero's *Consolatio Ad Se*: Character, Purpose, and Impact of a Curious Treatise." In Han Baltussen (ed.), *Greek and Roman Consolations. Eight Studies of a Tradition and Its Afterlife.* Swansea: Classical Press of Wales, 67–92.

Blacklock, Thomas. 1767. *Paraclesis; Or Consolations Deduced from Natural and Revealed Religion: In Two Dissertations.* Edinburgh: J. Dickson and London: T. Cadell.

Curtius, Quintus (trans.). 2021. *Cicero: Tusculan Disputations.* Charleston, SC: Fortress of the Mind Publications.

# BIBLIOGRAPHY

Forsyth, R., Holmes, D. I., Tse, E. K., et al. 1999. "Ci
cero, Sigonio, and Burrows: Investigating the A
thenticity of the *Consolatio*." *Literary and Linguist
Computing* 14.3:375–400. doi:10.1093/llc/14.3.375.

Garisendus, Gratius Lodius (ed.). 1599. *Caroli Sigon.
Postrema Oratio pro Consolatione Ciceronis*. Bolo
gna: apud haeredes Io. Rosii.

Graver, Margaret R. 2002. *Cicero on the Emotions:
Tusculan Disputations 3 and 4*. Chicago: University
of Chicago Press.

Ignatieff, M. 2021. *On Consolation: Finding Solace in
Dark Times*. New York: Henry Holt and Company.

King, Charles W. 2020. *The Ancient Roman Afterlife:
Di manes, Belief, and the Cult of the Dead*. Austin:
University of Texas Press.

Klotz, Alfredus. (ed.). 1876. "Incerti auctoris Consolatio." In *M. Tulli Ciceronis Scripta quae manserunt
omnia* vol. 4.3. Leipzig: Teubner, 372–431.

Mangeart, Jules. (trans.). 1840. "Consolation." In
J. Pierrot et al., *Oeuvres Complètes de Cicéron*.
Paris: C.L.F. Panckoucke, 226–438.

McCuaig, William. 1989. *Carlo Sigonio: The Changing
World of the Latin Renaissance*. Princeton, NJ: Princeton University Press.

Vitelli, Claudius. 1979. *M. Tulli Ciceronis Consolationis
Fragmenta*. Milano: A. Mondadori.